CU00705372

BEGINNER'S GUIDE

PAINTING IN

Gouache

PATRICIA MONAHAN

STUDIO
VISTA

ACKNOWLEDGEMENTS
The author and publisher would like to thank the following
artists, who have allowed us to use their work in this book:
Kate Gwynn, Brenda Holtam, Adrian Smith, Stan Smith and William Taylor.
Special thanks are also due to Winsor & Newton for technical
advice and their generous help with materials; to Stan Smith for
advice and assistance; and to Fred Munden for taking the photographs.

Studio Vista
A Cassell imprint
Villiers House
41/47 Strand
London WC2N 5JE

Text copyright © Jenny Rodwell and Patricia Monahan 1993
Volume copyright © Cassell Publishers Limited 1993

All rights reserved.
No part of this publication may be reproduced or transmitted in any form or by any
means, electronic or mechanical, including photocopying, recording or any
information storage or retrieval system, without prior permission in writing from the
publishers.

First published 1993

British Library Cataloguing in Publication Data

A catalogue record for this book is available from the British Library

ISBN 0-289-80080-3

Series editors Jenny Rodwell and Patricia Monahan
The moral rights of the author have been asserted

Series designer Edward Pitcher

Distributed in the United States by
Sterling Publishing Co. Inc.
387 Park Avenue South, New York, NY 10016-8810

Typeset by Litho Link Ltd, Welshpool, Powys, Wales
Printed in Great Britain by Bath Colourbooks

CONTENTS

CHAPTER 1
GOUACHE, BODY COLOUR OR
    WATERCOLOUR   4
The advantages of gouache   6
The qualities of gouache   8
Approaches to gouache   10

CHAPTER 2
MATERIALS   12
Paints   14
Supports   16
Stretching paper   18
Brushes   20
Etc. . . .   22

CHAPTER 3
FIRST STEPS   24
Using paint   26
Laying a wash   28
Wet and dry effects   30
The quality of edges   32
Dark on light, light on dark   34
PROJECT: Honesty   36
Toning a ground   40
PROJECT: Hillside   42
PROJECT: Tulips   46
PROJECT: Tractor   50

CHAPTER 4
MORE TECHNIQUES   54
Creating textures   56
Resist   58
PROJECT: Crab   60
PROJECT: Shells   64

PROJECT: Daffodils   68
Masking   70
Using gum arabic   72
PROJECT: Lamp   74
PROJECT: Figure   78
PROJECT: Anemones   84
PROJECT: Skull   86
PROJECT: Farmhouse   88
PROJECT: Mill   92

Index   96

Gouache, body colour or watercolour

GOUACHE IS A thrilling medium, infinitely flexible, forgiving, kind to the beginner and easy to use. Why, then, haven't you heard of it before? There are several possible explanations.

Gouache is often associated with 'commercial' art, with the work of designers and illustrators. You might have noticed that most manufacturers describe it as 'designers' gouache'. I suspect that if you are unfamiliar with the medium you might take this literally and assume therefore that 'fine' artists are excluded. It may also be that gouache suffers in comparison with watercolour, a medium people are familiar with and perceive to be more glamorous. Finally, it may simply be that people don't know how to use it – certainly very little has been published on the subject.

So what is gouache? It is an opaque form of watercolour. In fact, by adding white paint to transparent watercolour you can create gouache effects. You may also have come across the term 'body colour', which is just another way of describing gouache.

In the study above, Stan Smith exploits the textural qualities of gouache, combining it with oil pastel and pencil to create a picture surface that is descriptive and at the same time entertaining. The windmill was painted on a buff-coloured paper which warms the blue of the sky and is allowed to stand for the timber of the building.

THE ADVANTAGES OF GOUACHE

The watercolour media can be confusing if you are not familiar with them. There are three popular types of paint which can be described as watercolour because water is the vehicle with which they are diluted and applied to the support. They are transparent watercolour, gouache and acrylic. I will describe them all briefly, so that you can see how they differ from one another. If you are familiar with acrylic or transparent watercolour, it will help if you understand how the medium you know differs from gouache. If, on the other hand, you know nothing about any of them, you have an advantage because you won't harbour preconceived ideas about which is better, or how they should be used.

Transparent or pure watercolour

Transparent watercolour – also known as pure watercolour or simply watercolour – is available as pans and tubes. It is painted on white paper, which shows through the transparent films of colour, giving it a special scintillating brilliance. White paint is not used with pure watercolour, because that would reduce the transparency which gives the medium its unique character, so the white of the paper is the only white available to the artist. The watercolour artist must be organized and make sure that the white of the paper is reserved in the correct areas for highlights and pale tones. Darker tones are created by adding less water to the paint, or by overlaying washes of colour. This method of working is described as 'working light to dark' and is an important concept.

Acrylic

Acrylic is also a watercolour medium but, unlike pure watercolour, it is opaque and dries to an insoluble film. It can be used in a thin, washy way on paper like watercolour or gouache, or it can be used like oil paint to build up thick impastos and

for large-scale work. It is sold in tubes and tubs, often in two consistencies, one fluid and the other creamy or paste-like.

Gouache

Gouache is an opaque form of pure watercolour, but that single difference entirely changes its character. If you overlay one opaque colour with another, you can obliterate the colour beneath. So, for example, you could lay down an area of black and apply patches of white 'highlights' over it. Immediately you can see that you have the ability to 'work from dark to light' – the reverse of the transparent watercolour process.

The dark-to-light procedure is much easier for the beginner to work with, as it is not necessary to decide at the very beginning of the painting where the whites and the lightest areas are going to be. It also makes gouache more 'forgiving', because if you make a mistake or change your mind you can simply overpaint, obliterating whatever went before.

A further advantage of gouache, following on from the medium's opacity, is that it can be used on coloured or tinted supports. This offers exciting opportunities and is particularly useful to the beginner, as painting on a toned ground is much easier than painting on white.

◁ *Gouache, pen and ink were used for this on-the-spot study by Stan Smith, on a recent visit to Venice.*

▽ *Adrian Smith is primarily a watercolourist, but the solidity of gouache allows him an alternative approach which is bolder and more direct.*

All the watercolour media share the advantage of requiring relatively simple materials: paper, paint and water. They are also quick-drying, which is convenient for working out of doors and for developing quite complicated works over a short period of time. Gouache and watercolour materials are easy to care for, as the paint remains water-soluble when dry, so palettes, brushes and paints can be cleaned with water, even when the paint has dried. (With acrylic, brushes are very difficult to clean once the paint has dried on them.)

▽ *Brenda Holtam used gouache on card for this study of Jubilee Market in London's Covent Garden.*

7

THE QUALITIES OF GOUACHE

Although many of the techniques are the same, gouache is nevertheless very different from watercolour. Watercolour gains a brilliance and brightness from the white of the paper, and has a vivid, dancing quality. Gouache has a pleasing bloom and a rather more studied and considered quality. But it can still be as fresh as a daisy.

Scale

Like watercolour, gouache is an intimate, immediate medium. It is generally used on paper, usually in relatively small sizes – up to 20 × 30 in (50 × 70 cm) – though artists like Edward Burra (1905–76) have used both watercolour and gouache on a much larger scale. Gouache can be used in the studio on large sheets of stretched paper, but it can also be used on small watercolour pads, so it is ideal if you are working away from home.

A range of techniques

With gouache you can exploit all the traditional watercolour techniques, laying down washes, working wet on wet and allowing the colours to melt, then applying crisper areas of paint on to dry surfaces. You can make good washes from opaque colour, though you'll find that some gouache colours, like viridian, are actually quite transparent.

Drying times are an important aspect of any medium, and not just for practical reasons. With gouache you can get the image and start playing with it in minutes rather than hours, giving a wonderful sense of immediacy. You can work in concentrated bouts, getting totally involved with the paint and the paint surface, laying down colour, seeing how it behaves, and then responding to that, so the process becomes part of the finished image.

You can have marvellously fresh colours even with eight overlays. And because gouache is opaque you can exploit an almost limitless range of techniques. Paint can be applied with a plastic knife, a pen or any sort of brush. You can stipple, scumble or spatter the paint, or feather your brush and use a dry-brush technique. You can 'draw' into the wet paint, scratch back through the dry paint surface or even break the paper surface with a blade to create texture. You can work wet on wet or wet on dry, light to dark or dark to light. You can leave the white of the support, as in watercolour, or add highlights with a touch of white at the very end.

Mixing media

Some of the most exciting results are obtained by mixing media. You can cover areas with candle wax or oil pastel and exploit the way it repels the watery paint. You can add linear details or textures with pencil, pastel, crayon or pen and ink, or combine it with collage.

△ 'Louise in the kitchen' by Brenda Holtam.

◁ 'East Fellside 2' by William Taylor.

▷ 'Landscape' by Adrian Smith. The artists use gouache to create entirely different moods in their paintings. Each has a unique way of handling the paint and creates a picture surface that is expressive and personal.

APPROACHES TO GOUACHE

One of the features which recommends gouache to the beginner is that it allows you, even encourages you, to work in a very direct and free way. For most people, even experienced artists, there are two major problems with painting: getting started, and finishing. Gouache makes both easier. Allow yourself to feel free, to relish the materials and to plunge in with a spirit of adventure. You will find that gouache is both easy and a joy to use.

Toning a ground

You will find it much easier to get started if you use a toned ground. This can be a sheet of either tinted paper or paper tinted with a wash of colour.

Start with a middle tone – nothing too positive or aggressive: yellow ochre, raw sienna and mid-blue are all good middle-order colours. The way to test whether you have got a mid-tone is to lay in the colour and then touch a bit of white on to one brush, a bit of black on to another, and hold the brushes over the two sides. If they both read well, you've got a mid-tone.

Any colour you choose will condition both the picture you make and your attitude to it, so avoid dull middle greys. The way we experience colours is affected by factors such as how they are lit, surface texture and the influence of adjacent colours. Leaden colours like battleship grey deaden subsequent paint layers, whereas a colour taken from the palette of the picture will provide a foil for the colours you lay on and will enliven overlying washes.

Why tone a support?

There are many ways in which a toned support is easier to work on, especially for the inexperienced painter. First of all, by using a mid-tone wash you will knock back the white of the support, which is a stark and demanding colour to work against. As soon as you lay other colours on to a toned ground you begin to see relationships rather than separate colours, because the areas between the patches of paint have a positive and lively quality, and

contribute to the whole image. With a white ground, on the other hand, the colours retain their separateness and so it is much more difficult to 'see' them as part of a unity.

With a mid-tone, forms, spaces and distances become apparent as soon as you start to add lighter and darker tones. The image 'takes shape' so quickly that it can seem too easy – a bit of a cheat!

A mid-tone ground unifies a picture. Whatever

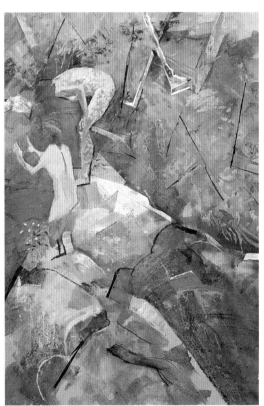

◁ *'The teapot' by Brenda Holtam. Because it is opaque, gouache can be used on a tinted support. For this painting the artist chose a greenish-grey card. The paint is applied freely and directly, built up from a web of hatched strokes which give the painting a shimmering quality. The colour of the support contributes to the painting, especially in the background.*

you do it always has some coherence, because the underlying colour qualifies the overlying colours and pulls everything together.

It also suggests completion, because there are no 'empty spaces'; the background can be indicated with a few simple touches. With a white background, on the other hand, the white spaces will be a distraction, making it difficult to read the whole painting; they will have to be killed in some way — filled in or knocked back with a wash.

△ *'Figures by a pool' by Stan Smith. The artist worked on a mid-grey support which imbues the entire painting with a warm tone. This underlying colour provides a foil for the cool greens of foliage and water, and the greys of the rocks in the foreground. The artist has used a range of techniques, including collage, to capture the flickering quality of the dappled summer light, creating a picture which is descriptive, decorative and entertaining.*

11

Materials

ONE OF THE pleasures of painting is the sheer enjoyment of the materials. Even the humblest art shop is an Aladdin's Cave of marvels. There are tubes of oil, acrylic, watercolour and gouache in serried racks, cubes of watercolour set out invitingly like delicious sweets and paintboxes in plastic, metal and wood. Sheets of paper are stored in wide, shallow drawers: soft papers in subtle colours for pastel, glossy boards for illustration and thick, creamy, handmade watercolour papers with frilly deckle edges.

There is an unhurried air about an art shop and purchases are carefully considered: papers have to be handled and held up to the light; paints are selected, put back and taken down again. The materials are wonderfully seductive, but their range and very unfamiliarity can be daunting for a beginner. On the following pages I've suggested a kit of materials to get you started, but you'll soon add to them.

Buy a catalogue from one of the large manufacturers. This is an excellent way of familiarizing yourself with what is available. A hand-painted colour chart is also an invaluable tool.

PAINTS

Gouache is a concentrated paint with a high tinting strength, brilliant matt colour, high opacity and great covering power.

The colours are generally available as semi-fluid paint in 14-ml metal tubes, but black and white, which are used a lot, come in larger sizes – generally 37-ml tubes or 100-ml pots. Winsor & Newton also produce a range of twelve solid discs. Gouache is a popular medium with commercial artists, such as those who work with airbrushes, graphic designers and illustrators, though acrylic is also popular for these applications. The range of colours varies from manufacturer to manufacturer, but Daler Rowney have a choice of 90 and Winsor & Newton 120. Colours like copper, silver and gold are aimed at the commercial artist, but some intended for designers, like the warm and cool greys, can be useful to the fine artist.

Price

There is more information on a tube of paint than just the colour and the quantity. Particularly useful to know is the 'series number'. Paints vary in price, because some pigments are more difficult to obtain than others. To avoid pricing each colour separately, manufacturers have grouped them into series. To find the price of a particular colour, look at the series number on the tube, then check the price on the published price list or on the price ticket in the shop. Daler Rowney divide their colours into Series A–D, with A being the cheapest, while Winsor & Newton's series runs from 1 to 4, with 1 being the cheapest.

Permanence

Pigments vary in their degree of permanence – that is, the length of time and the conditions in which they will retain their colour. For Winsor & Newton the system is as follows:

AA extremely permanent colour
A   durable colour
B   moderately durable colour
C   fugitive colour

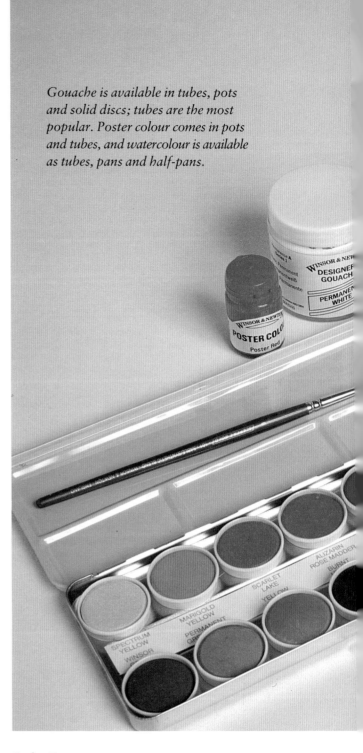

Gouache is available in tubes, pots and solid discs; tubes are the most popular. Poster colour comes in pots and tubes, and watercolour is available as tubes, pans and half-pans.

Daler Rowney use a star system:

**** permanent
*** normally permanent
** moderately permanent
* fugitive

Opacity and staining power

Pigments vary in their covering power. Some, like Winsor & Newton's permanent white, are completely opaque, whereas others, like lemon yellow, are fairly transparent. Look at the manufacturer's catalogue for information on each colour. Some

manufacturers also indicate the colour's staining power – the degree to which it will stain the support or other colours.

Poster colour
This is a cheaper form of opaque watercolour which is usually available in pots, though sometimes in tubes. Occasionally used for commercial work, poster colours are popular with children and schools.

Body colour
This is another name for gouache or opaque watercolour, but it is often used to describe opaque watercolour created by adding white paint to transparent watercolour.

Watercolour
Gouache, poster colour and acrylic are all forms of watercolour, but the term 'watercolour' in normal usage is reserved for transparent watercolour. This is available in tubes and semi-moist pans and half-pans. Watercolour is made opaque by the addition of white paint and is then described as 'body colour'.

SUPPORTS

Gouache is opaque and can therefore be used on coloured papers and boards – unlike pure water-colour, which can be used successfully only on a white or very pale support. Used thickly, straight from the tube, gouache will completely obliterate the support, but when it is diluted with water it becomes more transparent and the coloured ground will show through and modify the overlying paint layer. This offers marvellous opportunities to play games with the colour and texture of the support and the colour and transparency of the paint.

Hot-pressed, 'not' and rough

Watercolour paper is designed to take a water-based paint, so it is easy to use. Machine-made watercolour paper is available in three kinds of surface: hot-pressed, 'not' and rough. Hot-pressed paper has a smooth surface, created by passing it through heated rollers in the paper mill. 'Not' or cold-pressed paper, which has a rougher surface, is passed through cold rollers, so it is 'not' hot-pressed. Hand-made papers have a range of wonderful surfaces which are a pleasure to use but, as you might expect, they are costly.

Good watercolour papers are sealed with size on the painting side. This provides a good receptive surface for wet paint. If you buy paper as single sheets you can find the painting side by looking for the watermark. This is the maker's name, which is impressed into the paper during the manufacturing process. To see it, hold the paper up to the light – the name will be right-reading on the painting side.

The paper you choose will depend on personal taste and on the purpose for which it is to be used. While a hot-pressed paper will be ideal for detailed work, it doesn't have much tooth and you may find

it too slippery. The way the paint responds to the irregular surface of a rough paper is exciting, with the colour puddling in the recesses and running off the higher areas to create a lively, sparkling surface. Start with a cold-pressed, medium-textured paper – this combines an absorbent, toothy surface with a sympathetic texture. Choose a large pad of Winsor & Newton's Cotman watercolour paper. Either side can be used – they differ slightly but both are 'not'.

Paper weights

Papers vary in thickness and density, which is expressed as weight per ream (500 sheets), or grammes per square metre (gsm). Most watercolour papers fall within a range of 90 lb (185 gsm) to 300 lb (640 gsm). To start with, choose a 140 lb (300 gsm) paper and get into the habit of stretching it. This prevents the paper cockling when successive wet washes are applied.

Sheets, pads and blocks

Paper is sold by the sheet and in pads or blocks of various sizes. Blocks and pads are convenient for sketching and for working out of doors; pads which are glued on four sides are particularly useful, as the paper doesn't need to be stretched.

Other supports

Almost any paper or card, including cheap materials like wrapping paper and cardboard, can be used with gouache. The thinner papers should be stretched. If papers are too absorbent, they can be sealed with paper size. Purchased in jars, this is warmed and brushed on to the paper. Acrylic media can also be used to size the paper. Experiment with different papers – you'll soon find the ones you like.

Here we show a selection of papers suitable for gouache. They include hot pressed, 'not' and rough surfaces, and a selection of tinted papers.

TECHNIQUES

STRETCHING PAPER

Many watercolour techniques involve flooding the paper with water. Paper stretches when wet and shrinks as it dries. The degree to which this occurs depends on the amount of water used, the weight and composition of the paper, and whether or how it is sized. Unfortunately, paper doesn't usually dry flat but buckles and wrinkles. I'm sure as children we've all experienced the disappointment and frustration of seeing our work of art become distorted and misshapen, with water pooling in the recesses. To avoid this, all lightweight papers, especially those which aren't designed for use with watercolour, should be stretched on boards and allowed to dry before you start painting. This might seem a bit of a performance, but once you get used to it, it becomes a simple and satisfying process.

To make sure you always have stretched paper to hand when you need it, stretch several sheets at a time. You will need a supply of wooden drawing boards, or you can make your own from cheap offcuts of plywood or medium-density fibreboard (mdf) – a couple of coats of varnish will render them waterproof. Don't use hardboard, as it isn't strong enough and bends as the paper dries.

Leave the paper gummed to the board as you paint. When the painting is finished and dry, it can be cut from the board using a metal straight-edge and a craft knife.

△ **1** *You will need a drawing board, thick plywood or any other smooth surface, plus gummed paper, water, scissors and a sponge.*

△ **2** *Place the paper on the board right side up and cut four strips of gummed paper to the required length. Have a bowl of water close to hand. Wet the paper using the sponge. Work quickly, spreading the water across the paper – it should be wet but not soaking. Smooth the paper with your palm, but don't pull it.*

▷ **3** *Wet the strips of gummed paper.*

▽ **4** *Place the gummed strips along the edge of the paper. Leave the paper to dry naturally.*

BRUSHES

A brush is more than a tool for applying paint to the support; it is a means of expressing yourself, an extension of your arm, an important part of the creative process. Some brushes are just right for a specific job – a rigger for drawing a long, thin line, for example; others you simply like and feel comfortable with. Some seduce by their appearance: for example, I've got a Pro Arte mop with a wire-bound ferrule that I love because it's such a beautiful object.

Good brushes are expensive. They must be chosen with care and well looked after. Wash your brushes with soap and water at the end of every session, making sure you get all the paint out of the area near the ferrule. Flick them into shape, or shape them with your fingers. Leave them to dry fibre end up in a jar and never store them on their bristle ends.

Natural fibres

For gouache or watercolour you will need soft-fibre brushes. These are designed to hold dilute paint and are used to lay down watercolour washes and glazes of thin, transparent colour, and for fine line and detailed work.

The best, and most expensive, brushes are made from sable. The sable is a marten found in central and northern China and parts of Russia. The very best brushes are made from the hairs of the Kolinsky sable, which is found in parts of Manchuria and Siberia. These are the most expensive brushes of all and if you acquire one you should cherish it.

Sable has a special springiness and an ability to hold paint and retain a fine point, qualities which have always recommended it to watercolourists. Other natural materials used for brushmaking include ox hair, taken from the ear of the animal, and squirrel.

Ox is coarser than sable and doesn't make a good point, so it is generally used for one-stroke and large brushes, where a point is not important. Squirrel doesn't have the springiness of sable, but as it is less expensive it is often used for large wash brushes and craft work.

Synthetic brushes

Plastics technology now provides us with an excellent range of synthetic brushes. Some of these are very good, and they are certainly cheaper than sable. Some of the best value-for-money brushes are made from mixed fibres.

Sizes

Brush sizes are expressed as a series of numbers: 000 is generally the smallest and 14 or 16 the largest. Ranges of brushes of a particular quality are usually referred to as a series. A number 6 in one series will not be exactly the same as a number 6 in another, and sizes will also vary from manufacturer to manufacturer.

Shapes

Brushes consist of the hairs and a metal ferrule which grips them and attaches them to the handle.

The ferrule may be round or flat and the handle may be long or short. Different brush shapes give you a range of different marks. Round brushes are probably the most flexible: they hold a lot of colour and can be used to colour a large area. The point can be used to draw a fine line, but if you exert pressure you can also create a swelling line. Flat brushes are useful for broad strokes of colour and are sometimes called one-stroke brushes. However, you can make different marks using the side of the brush or the tip. Riggers have long, slender hairs and are used for drawing thin lines. Fans are used for delicate blending and mops are used for washes.

Selecting brushes

When buying a round sable or synthetic brush, you need to see if it retains its shape when wet. A good brush should come to a neat point, with no stray hairs sticking out. Art shops provide a pot of water so that you can test if it does. Dip the brush in the water and then give it a vigorous flick. It should return to its correct shape.

Start with three round brushes in different sizes, choosing one that is much larger than you think you can handle. A big brush will be useful for wash techniques and will encourage you to work boldly. The Winsor & Newton Sceptre range of mixed sable and synthetic fibres is excellent – sizes 1, 6 and 14 will give you a good start.

A selection of Winsor & Newton brushes. Left: sable and synthetic blend; sable; hog fan; ⅜in (1cm) one-stroke brush. Right: Cotman 2in (5cm) synthetic wash brush; sable rigger; synthetic; large sable and synthetic blend.

ETC....

To paint in gouache all you really need is some paint, a brush, a support, a pot of water and somewhere to mix your colours. But there are lots of other things you *could* have. I'll run through them quickly.

Media

There are various media you can add to gouache to change the way the paint behaves. Gum arabic and gum water makes gouache more viscous, transparent and glossy. It can be worked in to create patterns and textures. Watercolour medium improves the flow of the paint, and there are also media like Winsor & Newton's Aquapasto or Daler Rowney's Water Colour Impasto Gel, which thickens the paint and enable you to create an impasto effect.

Oxgall increases the wetting and flow of the paint, and makes it more transparent. And remember, any medium which can be used with watercolour can also be used with gouache.

Masking fluid

Masking fluid is used to protect or 'mask' paper from washes of colour.

Easels

There are various kinds of easels, some wooden, some metal and some portable, plus solid studio easels intended for large-scale work. To use washes successfully and make the most of the medium, you will need to work on a table, though you may want to do large works at a studio easel. You should be able to use a sketching easel in a horizontal position, so that washes can be laid easily.

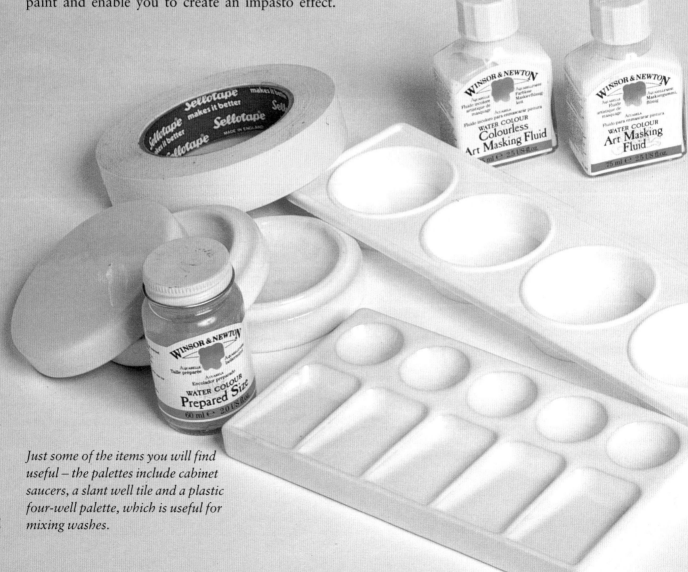

Just some of the items you will find useful – the palettes include cabinet saucers, a slant well tile and a plastic four-well palette, which is useful for mixing washes.

Drawing boards

You can never have too many boards. You will need them for stretching paper, and heavy paper can be pinned or clipped to the board. You can make your own boards by varnishing plywood.

Palettes

You will need a palette on which to lay out your paints and somewhere to mix washes. A white surface is most suitable, as it allows you to see the colour of the paint. However, this could just as well be a white ceramic dinner plate or a large plastic tray. If you keep your paints in a metal or plastic paintbox, the lid will have wells in it to hold paint, and there may even be an extra flap which folds out. This arrangement is particularly useful if you paint out of doors, as it means you have fewer things to carry.

In the studio you will probably want more space for mixing. Palettes may be plastic or ceramic, in a variety of shapes and sizes. Individual mixing dishes, again plastic or ceramic, give you more space for mixing larger washes. Saucers will do equally well.

Bits and bobs

You will soon collect your own bag of tricks, but clean cotton cloths, natural sponges and kitchen paper are essential. Buy a big sponge from the chemist and cut it into the sizes required, rather than buying the tiny but expensive sponges on sale in art shops. You will soon find yourself hoarding glass jars. Masking tape is useful and gummed paper is needed for stretching paper. A plastic palette knife is useful for mixing paint, and also for creating textures. You'll need a dip pen and drawing ink for pen-and-ink techniques. Gouache is wonderful for mixed-media techniques. In the projects here we've combined it with collage, pastel, pencil and resist, so you will need glue, a selection of soft pastels, oil pastels, pencils and a candle.

First steps

*I*N THIS CHAPTER I describe and illustrate some of the ways in which gouache can be used. Equip yourself with plenty of scrap paper, paints, brushes, water and mixing dishes. Experiment with the techniques described, trying each one several times. Work freely on a large sheet of paper, don't throw anything away and, above all, enjoy what you are doing.

If something doesn't work, don't worry. Leave it and have another look at it later. Even if it is not what you intended, it may nevertheless be useful, interesting or beautiful. Allow yourself to make mistakes and be prepared to accept and exploit accidental effects.

The techniques are demonstrated and expanded in a series of step-by-step projects. I have described the process so that you can 'look over the shoulder' of a professional artist at work. Don't copy these pictures. You will learn much more by finding an equivalent subject of your own and exploring the process in your own way. In that way you will find your own unique language.

In this painting by Stan Smith the background spaces divide the picture area into bold geometric shapes which have an abstract simplicity and provide a foil to the flamboyant curves and vivid colours of the lobster. Notice the way the artist uses texture to enliven the picture surface.

TECHNIQUES

USING PAINT

The excitement and variety of gouache come from the way the colour behaves when mixed with water. Paint can be diluted with large quantities of water, so that it barely tints the paper, but if the same colour is thinned with less water you will achieve a darker, denser wash. More colour can be added to wet colour on the support, where it will flow and spread – the extent to which it does so will depend on how wet the support is and how wet the paint being added is.

There are also some dry-brush techniques – for example, by removing most of the mixed paint from the brush by dabbing it on tissue, you will achieve a scratchy, dryish effect. Paint can on occasion be used direct from the tube, but it may crack and peel off the surface unless you add a suitable medium. However, it is true to say that if you are going to get the most out of gouache – or watercolour, for that matter – you must learn to handle mixtures of water and paint.

I'm emphasizing this because far too many beginners seem to think that the jar of water is simply for cleaning their brushes. They are frightened of having too much water around because it seems uncontrollable and they think they'll get into a mess. Water is the vehicle which carries the colour and distributes it over the support in infinitely varied and beautiful ways – it is an essential part of the creative process.

Experiment
Collect lots of glass jars, palettes, mixing dishes or old saucers. Also equip yourself with as much scrap paper as you can lay your hands on, so that you can practise mixing colour and creating different effects.

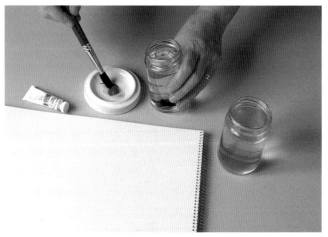

Using tube colour
△ **1** *Squeeze a dab of paint on to a mixing dish.*

▷△ **2** *Add enough water to make a wash. The more water you add, the paler the wash.*

▷ **3** *Test the intensity of the colour on a piece of paper. If it is too dark add more water, too light then add more paint.*

Watercolour and gouache change colour as they dry, becoming lighter, so you will have to learn to allow for this. With practice you'll find this becomes second nature.

A limited palette

Start with a limited range of colours. In the first place, this will save you money; second, it will force you to explore the possibilities of those colours, so that you learn about colour mixing; and third, if you use only a few colours and make your own mixtures from them, your paintings will have an inherent harmony.

A palette for landscape

You will need different palettes for landscape and for figure work. Landscape calls for a range of greens. These can be mixed from blue and yellow, but it is important to remember that there are lots of yellows, including the brownish yellows like yellow ochre and raw sienna. A palette for landscape should include ivory black, permanent white, cobalt blue, cerulean blue, Prussian blue, yellow ochre, cadmium yellow pale, raw umber and alizarin crimson.

A palette for figure work

For figure and portrait painting you require an entirely different mood. The earth colours give you a lovely range of flesh tints. Yellow ochre with light red gives you a subtle, resonant pink; yellow ochre with cobalt gives you the soft, natural green you often find reflected in flesh; and alizarin crimson and cobalt blue make an elegant lilac or a warm blue. Raw umber and cobalt give you another rich, rather sonorous green. And because you are using gouache, you can break down these mixes with white to create a whole range of subtle tints. A palette for flesh tones should include permanent white, cobalt blue, yellow ochre, burnt umber, oxide of chromium (green), light red and alizarin crimson.

◁△ **4** *Clean the brush in a jar of water.*

◁ **5** *Wipe the brush on a cloth before taking up another colour.*

△ **6** *You will need two jars of water, one for cleaning the brush, and another of clean water for diluting the paint.*

TECHNIQUES

LAYING A WASH

The ability to lay a flat wash is a basic skill. Flat washes are used for backgrounds and for expanses of flat uniform colour. Often, however, a variegated wash is more useful – with skies, seas and landscapes, for example. But practise laying a really flat wash first

– it is a good way of learning how the paint handles and how it changes as it dries. Experiment with different colours – you'll find that some are more transparent than others.

To lay a flat wash
Have several sheets of paper stretched on boards. You will also need paint, water, a large brush, a sponge and a mixing dish. There are a few useful tips to remember. First, start by mixing plenty of colour. You don't want to get half-way through laying the wash and find that you've run out, as it is

Laying a wash for a sky
△ 1 *Make an outline drawing of a landscape. Mix up a wash of cobalt blue and a wash of yellow. With a brush and clean water wet the paper up to the horizon line, working carefully around the details.*

extremely difficult to mix a wash of exactly the same tone and while you are fiddling about your wash may start to dry, creating irritating tidemarks where you don't want them. Second, make sure you have a brush which is the right size for the area you want to cover. You need to get the colour down before the paper starts to dry, so that you are working wet paint on to a wet surface throughout.

Start by dampening the paper with a sponge. Load the brush with colour, then tip the board at a shallow angle – about 10 degrees. Begin at the top left and take the brush across to the right. The paint will run down the slope and gather at the bottom of the painted band. Reload your brush if necessary and lay another band of colour, travelling from right to left and picking up the wet colour from the first band as you go. Repeat this until you have covered the required area. Collect the excess colour from the final band with a dry brush – otherwise it will be darker than the rest and the puddled colour will create tidemarks. Work briskly.

In practice, you very rarely need an absolutely flat wash, so don't worry if yours looks a bit uneven and patchy. But do persevere – you need to learn how to handle wet paint confidently.

◁ **2** *Turn the drawing upside down and tip the board. Load a brush with the yellow mix and flood it into the wet area along the horizon. The colour will flow down, away from the horizon. Pick up some of the blue and lay it below the yellow so the two colours melt together. Take the blue on down the page so you have a dense blue at the bottom. Work quickly to avoid the paint drying with a hard edge.*

△ **3** *To create a cloudy effect, drop in some white paint before the sky dries, adding darker tones for the underside of the clouds. Then allow the wash to dry naturally and flat.*

29

TECHNIQUES

WET AND DRY EFFECTS

Gouache is a remarkably flexible medium, but there are two main approaches to the application of paint, each of which creates an entirely different range of effects.

This image was painted on wet paper. The colour flowed freely, creating soft edges and gently modulated tones. Working in this way can be alarming as you cannot predict exactly how the paint will behave.

Wet on wet

Wet on wet describes applying paint to a wet or damp surface. This could be paper which has been dampened with water – as for the wash on the previous page – or it could be paper which has been dampened with a wash of colour. Wet-on-wet techniques are unpredictable. The apparent lack of control can be alarming, but these techniques are exciting and produce some of the loveliest and most useful effects. With experience you will learn how to exploit them.

A painting which was done entirely wet on wet would have no hard edges. Wet on wet is used for certain stages of a painting, or for particular areas,

often with crisper wet-on-dry passages applied on top.

The wetness of the paper will affect the way the paint behaves. The wetter the paper, the more random the effects and the less control you have. So on very wet paper the colours will bleed and run,

The second image was painted on to damp paper so that the colours melted into one another, but in a more controlled way.

In the third version on the right paint was applied to dry paper, creating a crisper image with hard edges. Find a similar subject and explore the possibilities of all three approaches.

sometimes with amazingly beautiful results. On barely damp paper, lines and edges will be softened.

Wet on dry

In wet-on-dry techniques paint is applied to a dry surface – this could be pristine paper or a painted but dry surface. Wet-on-dry techniques are generally much easier to control – the paint retains the shape of the brushmark and doesn't run away from you. Wet-on-dry techniques can be just as bold and vigorous as wet-on-wet – you can apply lots of colour boldly with a big brush, for example. But they can also be neat and precise, allowing you to paint fine details.

THE QUALITY OF EDGES

The quality of edges is an important element in painting. Crisp edges and clean lines can be used for accurate descriptions and to create sharp contrasts. Blurred edges, softly blended colours and tones, and gentle gradations from one colour to another have an entirely different impact.

Aerial perspective
Aerial perspective is a way of implying space in a painting by using warm and cool colours and contrasts of tone and focus.

Cool colours like blue tend to recede, while warm colours move to the front of the picture plane. By using cooler colours in the background of a landscape and warmer colours in the foreground you can suggest recession.

You can reinforce this by using tones which are close together in the distance, with more contrast between the lights and darks in the foreground. In the same way objects in the distance will be blurred or sketchily defined, while those in the foreground will be in sharp focus. Gouache allows you to create these contrasts of focus by exploiting wet-on-wet and wet-on-dry techniques.

If, for example, you are painting a rolling landscape, a series of washes can be applied wet on wet for the foreground, middle distance and background. This can be done boldly, loosely and fast. Details such as trees and hedges can then be

added to the still-damp surface. When the surface is dry, you can add crisp details in the foreground, bringing that area into focus and at the same time pushing the background back.

Mood

The treatment of edges affects the mood of a painting. Softly blurred forms and melting colours are atmospheric and evocative, while crisp edges and a controlled paint surface tend to be used for literal descriptions. All these effects are possible with gouache and can be exploited in your work.

In this broadly rendered but atmospheric image, softly blurred areas worked wet into wet are overlaid by crisp details applied wet over dry. In the foreground and middle distance crisply applied paint, linear detail and texture give the painting focus and pull it forward, while the overlapping watery washes in the background settle back into the distance. The predominantly cool colours in the background contrast with the warmer earth tones in the foreground, emphasizing the sense of space.

DARK ON LIGHT, LIGHT ON DARK

This is the area in which gouache differs from transparent watercolour.

Dark on light

In watercolour the only white you have access to is the white of the support. Lighter tones of a colour are created by diluting the colour with water. Darker tones are created by adding more colour, by building up layers or by adding black. The lightest tones are in those areas where the white of the paper is most visible. In the darkest areas the white

of the support is almost obliterated. This transparency gives good watercolours a special clarity and luminosity, but means that it is quite a difficult medium to use because you have to think in reverse.

Gouache offers you some of these possibilities in that it can be diluted to create semi-transparent washes, and with some especially transparent colours like viridian and cadmium you will be able to create fully transparent washes. And if you are working on a white support you can leave parts white to stand for highlights. The method of working in which darker tones are built up on paler tones is described as working dark on light.

Light on dark

If you think about it you'll realize that you can overpaint dark tones only if you use a paint with high opacity. Imagine a green glass bottle with lots of bright, sparkling highlights. With gouache you could lay down the bottle in shades of green, flood

The image on the left is painted dark over light. If you look carefully you will see that the stalks of the toadstools and the white spots on their caps are created by leaving the white of the paper to show through. Even the stems of the grasses are pale washes defined by darker patches of colour.

The image on the right is painted light over dark. Here all the white and pale elements are created with white and light-coloured gouache.

in white to create areas of pale green and then, when the painting was dry, put in patches of solid white as highlights. With watercolour, on the other hand, you would have to make sure that you left the paper untouched in the highlighted areas and gradually build up the tones elsewhere.

Again, imagine you want to create a range of reds, from bright red through to pale pink. In gouache you would do that by adding increasing amounts of white to the red paint. Of course, if you were working on a white support you could also dilute the red with water to create a different range of pale tones.

The advantages of gouache

With gouache you can work both dark on light and light on dark, which means it is a marvellously flexible medium, with almost limitless opportunities for inventiveness. Its other great advantage is that it allows you to use tinted papers, further increasing its flexibility.

HONESTY

This study provides an excellent opportunity to explore the concept of light on dark and dark on light. While the seed heads are painted with light paint over the tinted ground, the area of the table illuminated by sunlight is created with a pale wash of colour so that the white paper shows through and captures the brightness of the sunshine.

Gouache is an ideal medium for this study – it would be difficult to achieve the softly textured quality of the honesty, combined with the strong contrasts of the shadows, in pure watercolour. Gouache is, in many ways, more flexible and more forgiving. It allows you to overpaint, to lay paler, lighter colours over dark, cutting back into a darker passage.

Pure watercolour can be combined with gouache, and in fact is often the underpinning of a gouache painting. You can start with washes of transparent watercolour, working over it with body colour or gouache. This project also shows the way in which the abstract qualities in an obviously figurative subject can be explored and exploited. The leaves look white, a powerful neutral foil for the blue vase, which sings away against the white. With the light behind it, the group becomes very rich. Subjects for the painter are not always obvious or dramatic, but you can make something from nothing. Here the bars of the window cast crisp, geometric shadows, which contrast with the softly clustered forms of the seed heads. By playing on these contrasts, it is possible to achieve a wonderful fusion of figuration and abstraction. This tension between the purely descriptive and the abstract results in painting which rises above mere illustration – it is more interesting to look at and, significantly, much more interesting to make.

△ **1** *The delicacy and apparent complexity of the frail seed heads of this honesty posed something of a problem. Where to start and how to render those fine details? To simplify the subject, try to see it as areas of light and dark tones.*

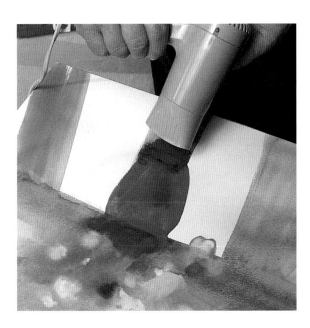

◁ **3** *A hairdryer is a surprisingly useful tool for the painter. Here it is being used to speed up the drying time. You can also use it to send a swirling line across a surface or to create a crisp edge.*

▽ **4** *The artist has used a limited palette of ochres, raw sienna, cobalt and white, loosely and broadly applied. The warms and cools balance and yet at the same time work against each other, as the warms push parts of the painting forward and the cools cause others to recede.*

▽ **2** *The artist, Stan Smith, started by tinting the paper with a mid-tone. He didn't lay on a flat wash but scrubbed in a general colour idea with a range of warm mid-brownish ochre colours, putting plenty of variation into it. He left the area where the light falls on the table white.*

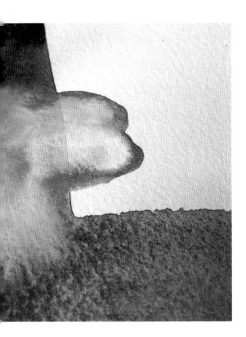

▷ 5 *Edges are an important aspect of a painting – a crisply drawn edge will have an entirely different feel to a soft one, and a ruled one will have a different feel to a drawn one. Crisp edges and contrasts also tend to come forward, while soft edges have a tendency to sit back in the space. Here the artist defines the edge of the table by laying on masking tape to create a neat, straight edge.*

◁ 6 *Avoid the temptation to draw the repeating forms of the honesty – the result would look obvious and heavy-handed. Here the artist has found a way of summarizing the forms using the round end of a felt-tip pen.*

◁ 7 *It is important to capture the quality of different materials without being too literal. Here a dry-brush technique is used to describe the grain of the planks of wood on the old-fashioned, scrubbed kitchen table. Load the brush with colour, then blot most of it off, squeezing the brush between your fingertips so that the fibres separate. Drag the brush lightly across the paper.*

▽ *The final painting captures the bright, light quality of the subject. It is descriptive but not slavishly realistic.*

△ 8 *The stems have been drawn with a fine sable brush loaded with a dark-brown paint. You don't need to depict every stem, and remember that those nearer the front will be crisper and bolder than those sitting behind.*

39

TECHNIQUES

TONING A GROUND

Because gouache is opaque you can use a coloured or tinted stock. One of the main reasons for doing this is quite simply that it is a very easy way of painting. If you choose a paper which has a useful mid-tone and lay in both light and dark tones, you'll find that the image begins to emerge surprisingly quickly. And the underlying mid-tone will modify the entire painting to some extent, pulling it together and giving it a sense of unity.

You can choose a mid-tone related to a useful local colour – blue for a seascape, green or ochre for a landscape, for example – but there are all sorts of games you can play. You could choose a colour which is a complementary of the predominant colour within the subject – red or terracotta for a green landscape, for example. Complementary colours appear opposite each other on the colour wheel and have a special relationship, one aspect of which is the way they enhance each other, so red, for example, will make green look richer. You could also play off warm and cool colours, using a warm stock for a predominantly cool painting and vice versa.

Toning the support

You can't always be sure that you will have paper of just the right colour to hand, but toning your own is easy and gives you more choice of colour and texture. To tone paper, follow exactly the same process as was described on page 28 for laying a wash. You stretch the paper, lay a wash of the appropriate colour and leave it to dry.

A toned ground gives you a splendid jumping-off point, and is especially useful for energetic and expressive pieces. To give it more interest, you can introduce a variegated, textured effect.

◁ **Toning with a brush**
Here a sheet of paper is toned with variegated colour using a brush. Choose a mid-tone which contributes to the image in some way.

▷ *Stan Smith conjured up the dappled light of a summer's day by first toning the paper with a wash of ochre, which imbues the subsequent paint layers with summery warmth.*

◁ **Toning with a sponge**
A sponge allows you to apply colour quickly and to large areas.

PROJECTS

HILLSIDE

The landscape provides the artist with an infinite source of stimulation and inspiration, but it can also seem difficult. In fact, there is nothing to beat painting out of doors, directly from nature.

The first problem that faces the novice landscape painter is the sheer enormity of the subject. Where on earth do you start when faced with views through 360 degrees, with landscape from your feet to the horizon and the dome of the sky above? A viewfinder – a rectangular frame cut from card – will help you isolate a rectangle of landscape. By holding it up to your eye and surveying the landscape through it, you can 'frame' the area that interests you. You can do exactly the same thing by making a frame using the thumbs and forefingers of both hands.

If you haven't tackled a landscape before, don't spend too much time trying to find the 'ideal' landscape – it is as elusive as the ideal picnic site. The best advice is, just get on with it, paint what you see, enjoy the materials and do not worry too much about the result. Nine times out of ten the result will be much better than you expect, even if it falls short of perfection.

Gouache is particularly suited to landscape painting. You can work fast, flooding on washes of colour to stand for foreground, middle distance and deep distance. You can drop in more colour, allowing it to bleed into the wet surface, creating softly blurred edges and variegated swathes of colour which match very closely the subtle, shimmering nuances of colour and tone in the landscape.

Once the surface has begun to dry, you can start to overlay more opaque colour and finally touch in the precise details which bring the foreground forward and pull the whole thing together.

This sketch was made quickly. The artist started working out of doors, adding the final touches later in the studio. He worked on a spiral-bound pad balanced on his knee. Watercolour pads are useful because they have a cardboard back which provides

firm support. Blocks are even better as they are gummed on all four sides – they are much firmer and the paper doesn't need stretching.

△ **1** *The artist started by tinting the paper with a mixed blue-grey wash. This captured the character of the scene and provided him with a useful middle tone to work into. While the paper was still damp he touched in a darker mixture of black and blue, allowing the colour to spread. Remember that gouache is darker wet than dry.*

▽ **2** *Here you can see that the sky, the distant hill and the middle distance have been indicated, but the forms are imprecise and the edges of the colour softly blurred. Keep the generalized feel, letting the colours melt, and enjoy the controlled randomness.*

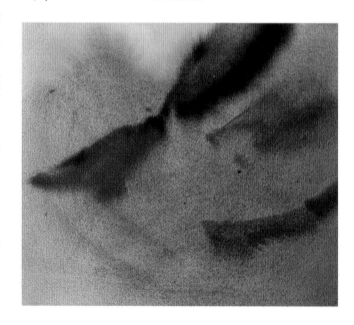

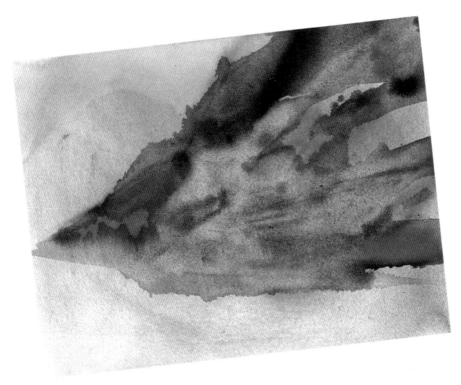

◁ **3** *Here you can see the way more colours have been let into the damp surface – raw sienna, ochre, viridian and Hooker's green, among others. Look for colours and tones, and paint what you see.*

▽ **4** *You can be quite inventive within the painting by letting the materials talk to you. So put a colour down and see what happens. If it doesn't contribute to the painting, blot it off. Even if the painting is dry, you can lift areas of colour by moistening them gently with a brush and blotting. While allowing the material some freedom, you must retain a basic sense of the forms and tonal values, and keep the colour consistent. In this case there is a pervading blue-greenness.*

▽ 5 *Gouache can be used with a variety of implements. Here a crisp line of colour is applied with a painting knife.*

◁ 6 *One of the problems encountered in landscape painting is how to create a sense of space and recession within the two dimensions of the support. This is especially difficult when you are dealing with an apparently amorphous subject, with few defined edges and no obvious structures or linear elements to give you a sense of scale. Aerial perspective is another way of resolving the problem. Here the artist has used warm earth colours in the foreground and cool blues in the distance. Crisp details, sharp contrasts and dark colours also tend to advance, so by defining the foreground and blurring the background you can imply receding space.*

◁△ 7 *The tinted paper stands for the foreground, which is a large part of the painting. In the studio the artist tightened up the foreground and placed it more firmly in space by adding this detail of clumps of vegetation.*

▽ 8 *To complete the painting the artist adds some touches here and there, but is careful not to lose the fresh, spontaneous quality of the paint.*

PROJECTS

TULIPS

Flowers are a delight to the eye and a joy to paint, their colours taken from the rich palette of nature and their shapes endlessly varied, from the fullness of overblown roses, to the spikes of irises and the densely packed florets of lupins and delphiniums. But their inherent charm and prettiness can be a trap, tempting the unwary into making a 'pretty' rather than a 'good' picture.

One way to overcome this tendency is to try and see the flower group as an abstract entity, a collection of lights and darks, colours and shapes, all with their own special personalities. When you have put together a group, study it carefully. Make up your mind about the qualities which attract you and focus on them. If your picture is to have any coherence you need a clear intention.

In this case, for example, there are many aspects which you could develop. If you look at the photograph of the group you will see that the flowers were in a stone jar, on a highly patterned cloth. This could provide you with your theme: the contrast between the fluid lines of the gracefully drooping flowers and the rigid geometry of the table. However, if you look at the final picture you'll see that the artist has simplified the image by editing out the pattern of the tablecloth.

In fact, one of the starting points of this project was the support. I had come across a pad of recycled paper in an art shop and rather liked the range of colours and the soft, matt texture. I asked the artist if he would experiment with it. We decided the paper would be too absorbent in its natural state so I sized it first. I used an acrylic medium rather than paper size, just to see what would happen. Don't be afraid to experiment. If things don't work well, it doesn't really matter – you'll have learnt something.

As it was, we found that the acrylic medium partly sealed the paper, while leaving it fairly absorbent. The artist exploited this quality in his painting.

◁ **1** *The tulips are a lovely subject, the flask-shaped flowers on their slender stems contrasting with the leafiness of the fleshy foliage. Tulips tend to droop, especially in the heat, so be prepared to make adjustments in your painting.*

▽ **2** *The artist drew the jar with a fine brush and a mixed grey paint – this allowed him to locate the group within the picture area. He then started to lay in the broad forms of the leaves with yellow and green, working wet on wet so that the colours flowed into one another. He laid a wash of light and dark tones for the jar and reds for the flowers.*

◁ **3** *The prepared paper has a lovely fresh quality. The priming of the paper retards the drying time and, though fairly absorbent, it doesn't suck up the colour too quickly. As a result the colour retains its freshness. At this stage you may feel that the painting is running away with you, but don't panic.*

▷ 4 *The painting was allowed to dry and then more opaque colour was laid on. The artist looks for the forms of the foliage, noting how the lights and darks are distributed across the surface, and how leaves are yellowy green where they catch the light and bluey green where they turn away from it. At this stage you must be prepared to let the image float away from you, confident that you can reclaim it later.*

△ 5 *Even at this stage the painting has all the best qualities of good gouache – the colour is clear and bright, with a pearly beauty which is entirely different from transparent watercolour.*

Notice the way the background has been simplified to focus attention on the central group. The table is reduced to a simple curve; the area beyond it painted blue so that it takes up a plane beyond the table.

▽ 6 *The painting is allowed to dry and the artist then adds more detail. Crisp lines define the leaves, and dark and light tones give solidity to the flower heads.*

▽ 7 One of the most valuable skills a painter can have is knowing when a picture is 'finished'. Unfortunately, you can learn this only by trial and error. Watercolour and gouache are particularly vulnerable to overworking, though gouache does allow you to overpaint and sometimes reclaim an apparently lost cause. Nevertheless, expect to 'lose' some good paintings.

Here the artist has judged the matter nicely, adding just enough detail for accurate description, while retaining the sense of excitement which was triggered by colours and shapes of the flowers. A painting must pick up the spirit of the subject and the artist's response to it.

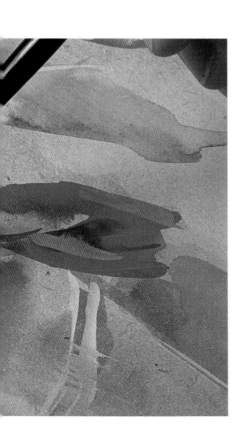

PROJECTS

TRACTOR

Here we have another out-of-doors subject, but one that presents entirely different problems from those encountered with 'Hillside' on page 42. There the problem was the huge vista and the lack of structural lines to hang on to. Here we have what seems to be a more complex topic, with the criss-cross tracery of the bare twigs and branches, the stone wall and the old Fergusson tractor and cultivator. The artist dealt with this by flooding in the colour, creating a key against which he could work. He looked for rhythms and patterns in the boughs and branches, paying as much attention to the spaces between them as to the trees themselves.

Never forget the quality of the paint surface, which is used to describe what is there but is also both a way of expressing a mood and an entertainment. You can see this if you look at some of the details of the painting.

The artist worked on a large scale, on a watercolour board, doing the bulk of the work out of doors. It was a complicated subject, so he worked on it over several days, allowing it to dry in between and returning to it at the same time of day. If you can afford the time, wait until the picture is totally dry – leave it overnight ideally – so that you can come to it afresh and make use of what you've got, including the happy accidents. You can mix entirely dry, damp dry and wet surfaces, exploiting the different qualities all three provide.

If you use dryish paint and don't overwork it, it shouldn't lift the paint below. If, however, it does, be prepared to incorporate the result in your painting. Take risks! Experiment!

Line was used to tighten up the drawing and to give it a special sparkling quality. These crisp details also help to establish the relative spatial arrangements, so that the twigs which come into the work at the front of the picture plane are more sharply focused than those in the distance, which are blurred. Try and think of the landscape as a series of overlapping planes, rather like a toy theatre with receding flats. Those in the front will be warmer and rendered in more detail; those furthest away will be most blurred and least clearly defined.

△ **1** *The subject is a challenging one. How can you establish a sense of space and deal with the complex tracery of leafless twigs and branches, the range of greens and the brilliant spring light?*

△▷ **2** *The drawing was made with a brush, using a mixed grey. Work boldly, making it fresh and free, with big areas of colour. Block in the darkest tone.*

▷ **3** *The artist started by blocking in areas of colour, trying to get the tonal relationships working, so that he had something to look at from a distance, assess and make judgements about. The colours used are cadmium yellow pale, Indian red and viridian.*

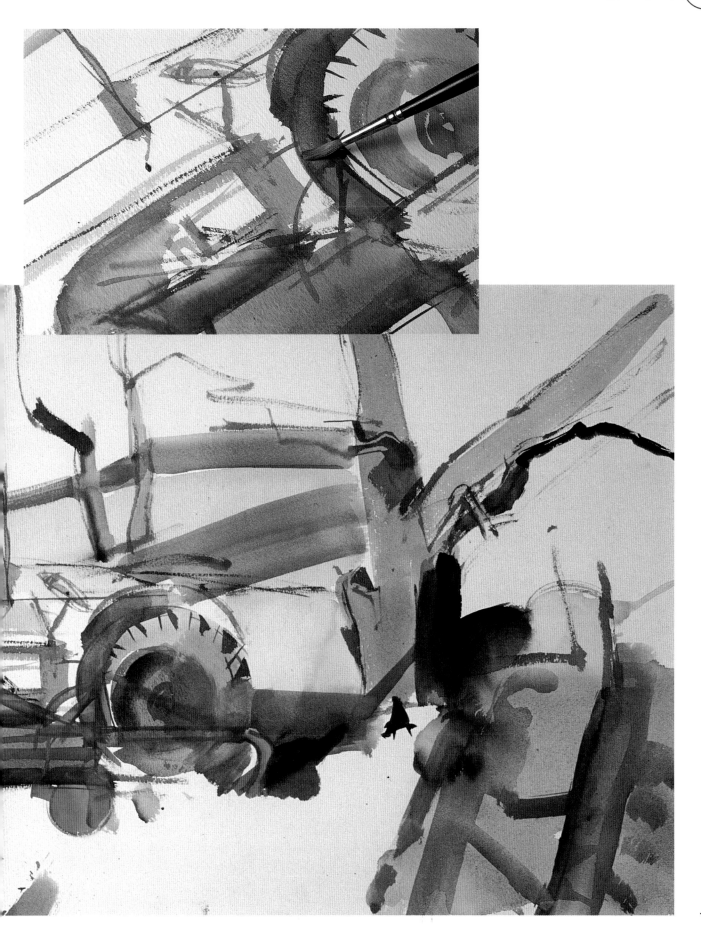

▷ **4** *He continues to develop the image, blocking in more colour, making adjustments, but keeping the whole picture surface working, and avoiding the temptation to focus exclusively on one aspect of the painting.*

△ **5** *This detail shows the way the image is interpreted as simple, bold strokes and patches of colour. In some areas the paint has become fairly opaque, almost obliterating the underdrawing, while in other areas the drawing still shows through. The artist started working wet on wet. When the painting became difficult to work, he left it to dry and added more colour wet on dry. Tree trunks, as in the full picture, are difficult to paint. If you draw them too precisely they will stand out too much and look unconvincing. A useful tip is to draw the negative of the branches – the spaces between them rather than the branches themselves. This is actually a very accurate way of drawing.*

▷ 6 *More colour is laid on. The blue hills in the background help establish a sense of distance, and push the rest of the painting forward. On the left a brownish wash is laid in to stand for a coppice of trees. This will provide a base for the artist to work on, adding more and more linear detail to describe the trunks, branches and twigs to create a picture which has a certain mood and sparkle.*

Greens are treacherous colours and can become muddy and undistinguished, or shrill. There are greens you mix from blues and yellows and also many proprietary greens. Experiment with mixes, looking for brown greens, yellow greens and blue greens to create a variety that reflects nature.

▽ 7 *The qualities that inspired this painting were the sparkling spring light, the rhythms of the boughs of the trees and the charm of the elderly tractor. The challenge was to make something of all of them, to create a pleasing design and reflect the mood of the scene.*

53

More techniques

TEXTURE IS AN important, and sometimes overlooked, aspect of painting. In this context we are describing as texture any broken paint surface, not just surface relief.

There are several reasons for introducing texture into a painting. It provides the artist with a useful and efficient means of creating a literal description of surface. You could, for example, use spattering to create a pebble beach, sgraffito for a thicket hedge and various stippled and sponged effects for sea and sky.

Texture can be used for purely decorative effect, to enliven the paint surface and delight the eye. It is also a powerful means of expression, a way of creating a mood in painting. Whereas a smooth, controlled surface, constructed from overlapping flat washes and orderly lines, will suggest calmness and serenity, a painting in which there are broken colours, agitated surfaces and jagged lines will create a sense of energy or even disharmony.

Stan Smith has devised a range of textures to describe the foliage of an orchard. He applied ink and paint with a variety of implements, finding an equivalent for what he saw while emphasizing the abstract and decorative qualities of the subject. Experiment with techniques and materials – but keep the paint surface fresh.

TECHNIQUES

CREATING TEXTURES

The effects you can create with gouache are almost limitless. To get the best from the medium you must get to know it, and the only way to do that is to practise. Spend as much time as you can experimenting on scraps of paper, and enjoy messing around with paint without the pressure imposed by trying to achieve a particular end. Play with the paint and see where it leads you.

Dabbing on and dabbing off
Mix some paint and try dabbing it on with a natural sponge, a synthetic sponge, a tissue, a nailbrush, the tip of a stiff brush, and anything else you can think of. See what images these textures suggest, and try overlaying different colours. Next lay down an area of colour and take colour off with a sponge, a tissue and a brush. Lay a wash of blue and take off paint with a damp sponge to create a cloudy-sky effect. Scrunched-up foil can be dabbed on to wet paint to create useful textures.

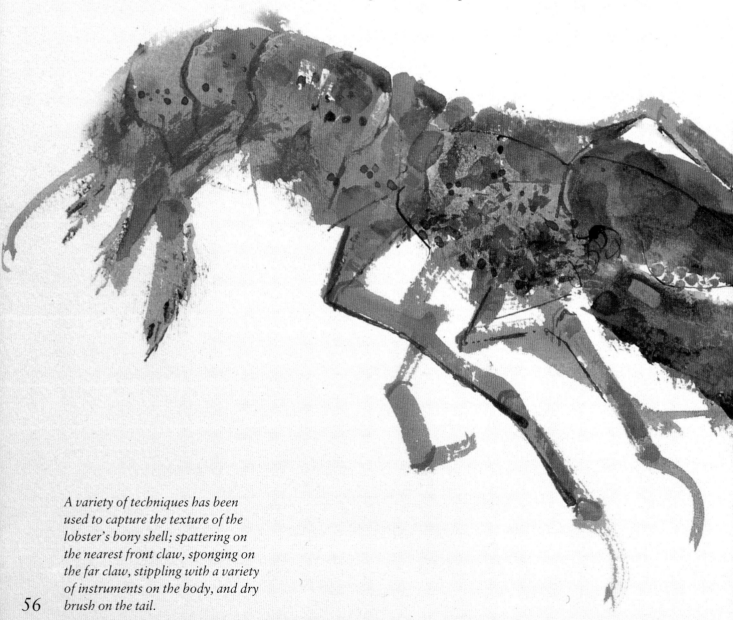

A variety of techniques has been used to capture the texture of the lobster's bony shell; spattering on the nearest front claw, sponging on the far claw, stippling with a variety of instruments on the body, and dry brush on the tail.

Spattering

Load a brush with water and flick the water on to an area of still-wet paint. The spatters of water will cause the colour to open up, creating pale blotches. This is a useful way of softening a passage which has become too harsh. Flick colour on with a loaded brush to create a splashy effect. Now pick up colour in a nailbrush or old toothbrush and run your finger briskly across the top of the bristles; the spray created will settle as a film of fine droplets. Explore what happens when you flick and spatter on to dry paper, damp paper and wet paper in turn.

▷ Spattering
Load an old toothbrush with colour, then run your thumb briskly across the bristles. A film of fine droplets will be deposited on the surface.

Dry brush

To create a dry-brush effect, dip the tip of a brush in colour and squeeze the bristles between your fingertips so that they are spread. Now drag the brush lightly across the paper surface to create a broken, scratchy effect. Working in the same way, apply another colour so that you create a complex web of different colours.

TECHNIQUES

RESIST

The resist techniques exploit the antipathy between oil and water. Candle wax, wax crayons or oil pastels can all be used to create a whole range of useful or beautiful textures. Again, set aside some sheets of paper and spend time experimenting with techniques. If you have a selection of different papers, so much the better. Cardboard and wrapping paper will be useful and provide pleasing textures and colours.

Using candle wax

Using an ordinary white domestic candle, apply wax to the paper surface. Experiment with different patterns – in one area lay down regular stripes of wax, in another scrub the wax on vigorously, working in different directions to create a complex pattern of lines. Now mix a wash of colour and apply it over the waxed areas, working boldly. Leave it to dry. The waxy areas repel the water, or most of it, so that they show as the colour of the paper modified by the film of wax, while the areas between take up the colour. Some of the paint won't be able to run off and will instead coagulate to form droplets which dry with a hard edge, creating yet another textural element.

Wax resist could be used to retain or to draw a

△ **Candle wax resist**
Colour is washed over a patch of candle wax which repels the water, causing it to run off or form droplets and allowing the white of the support to show through.

particular form. So, for example, if you were painting a birch wood, and working on a white or grey paper, you could lay in the trunks of the trees with slashes of wax and then apply a wash of green for the foliage. The waxed areas would show through as pale lines.

Oil pastel

The oil in the pastel repels water just as the wax of the crayon does, but in this case you have a range of colours to choose from. Again, experiment with different textures and different colour washes. Most oil pastels are softer than wax or wax crayons, so they handle differently to create a range of subtle effects.

△ Oil pastel resist
The oily surface of oil pastel or wax crayon rejects water in the same way as candle wax, but allows you to exploit colour contrasts at the same time.

▽ A candle wax resist is used to create the scaly texture on the head of the fish, while boldly applied oil pastel is used on its side and tail.

PROJECTS

CRAB

This project is an exercise in creating an image using a bold, direct approach. The crab was bought from a market stall. The artist was attracted by its rich colours, the horny nature of its shell and its bizarre, graphic shape. We experimented with the composition, placing the shellfish against different backgrounds, but the softly crumpled texture and creamy colour of the tissue paper provided the most satisfactory foil. The composition felt rather tame – too simple and too balanced. We tried adding a selection of different 'garnishes'. The lemon added the required zest – a touch of sharp colour and a geometric shape which perfectly balance the extra-ordinary outline of the crab.

The beauty of still life is the amount of control it gives you. You can arrange and rearrange the components; you can decide on the viewpoint and how the group will be lit. Often it is what you leave out of a painting as much as what you include that determines its success or failure. Much of this editing occurs in the painting process, but with a still life you can do quite a lot of the picture-making in the setting up.

The artist decided that a bold, vigorous approach would suit the subject. To achieve this he used a plastic palette knife and creamy paint for most of the work. He worked with a limited palette, allowing the white of the paper to stand for the creamy background, with hot reds and oranges for the crab and a cool yellow for the lemon. The perceived temperature of colours is relative, so this lemon yellow, which seems cool against the hot reds, would look warm against a chilly blue.

Set up a similar subject for yourself and have a go using this approach. But remember that there is no 'right way', so go on to do another painting of the same subject using an entirely different approach – perhaps something more delicate, with films of subtle washes and carefully worked detail.

△ **1** *Anything can be the subject of a painting. As a beginner, paint everything you can. Later, when you are more confident and competent, you may want to specialize. When you've selected a subject, contemplate it for a while so that you can absorb some of its qualities – whatever it was that caught your eye and makes it special. It is your response to the subject that is interesting, not just the skill with which you replicate nature. Here the obvious qualities are the vivid colours, the striking shapes, the texture of the shell and claws, and the spiny nature of the back claws. Keep these in mind as you paint.*

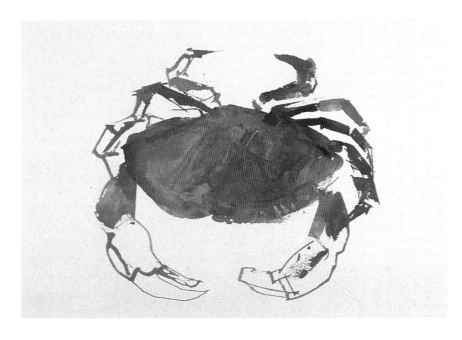

◁ **3** *Here you can see some of the ways the knife has been used. The flat of the blade was combined with a smearing gesture for the carapace, controlled gestures with the flat of the knife gave the solid colour in the limbs, and the side of the tip was used like a pen to draw the outlines elsewhere. Don't be afraid to experiment with tools and materials. This is undoubtedly the best way to learn and you may come up with something that really excites you.*

▽ **2** *A creamy mixture of spectrum red, cadmium yellow and crimson with a touch of white was smeared on to the support, creating a modulated, lively paint surface. The texture of the paper shows through the paint, giving it some of the character of the crab's shell. With the tip of his knife the artist 'draws' the limbs of the crab.*

△ **4** *With a brush loaded with cadmium yellow, the artist floods in colour.*

△ 5 *Here the artist is experimenting with a printing technique. He loads the cut surface of a lemon with yellow paint . . .*

▽ 6 *. . . and prints it on to the paper surface. This achieves two things. It leaves an imprint of the lemon, which can be developed later. It also introduces a different kind of mark, one which has less of the artist's hand in it.*

◁ 7 *Shadows and darker tones are laid in as simple washes using raw umber and a warm grey. The artist is at pains to avoid complicating the image in order to retain the freshness of his original concept. He paints the dark claws and, using the tip of the knife, indicates the creases in the paper.*

◁▽ 8 *The paint is allowed to dry and then, with a fine brush and dark paint, the artist adds enough crisp detail to pull the picture together.*

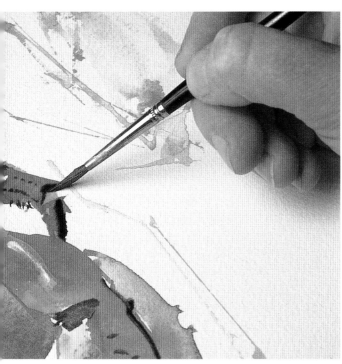

△ 9 *The finished image is simple but satisfying. Much of the picture is left as plain paper, with a few marks to indicate background.*

SHELLS

Keep your eye open for paintable subjects, not just in the time you have set aside for painting but as you go about your everyday business, say, or when you are out for an evening stroll. Have beautiful but generally overlooked objects about your home. Educate your eye to see the creative possibilities in the world around you. Painting is less about skill, manual dexterity and a knowledge of materials than you might think. Of course, those things help, but all the cleverness and trickery in the world won't compensate for an inability really to 'see'.

The seashore was the inspiration for this still-life study. Collect shells, pebbles, bits of driftwood and anything else that catches your eye. What fires you could be the marvellous spiralling shape of a shell, or the encrusted surface and bleached tones of a water-worn and salt-bleached piece of wood.

The subject presents a wonderful range of delicate muted tones which contrast with the delicious pink of the inside of the shell and the vivid yellow of the sponge. Shape provides another theme, the swirling spiral of the conch shell counterbalanced by the ribs of colour that define it. Against this we have the spiky murex, the knobbly texture of the coral and the compactly dappled form of the cowrie.

Stan Smith has chosen a high viewpoint which emphasizes the abstract qualities of the composition. Each of the objects is seen clearly in silhouette and this, together with the way you can read the sinous spaces between, draws attention to the shapes and patterns, rather than the identity of the objects or the way they are arranged in space. This flattens the whole composition and brings it nearer to the picture surface.

The strong black-and-cream pattern of the textile emphasizes the geometry of the composition and provides a nice contrast to the subtlety of the marine objects.

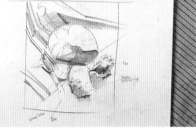

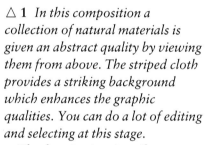

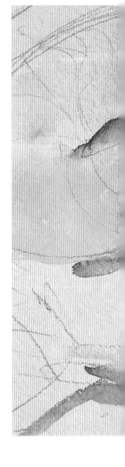

△ **1** *In this composition a collection of natural materials is given an abstract quality by viewing them from above. The striped cloth provides a striking background which enhances the graphic qualities. You can do a lot of editing and selecting at this stage.*

The drawing is primarily to assess the shapes and tones, so that you can make a relationship work within a rectangular space. At this stage keep the composition adjustable.

▷ **2** *The artist starts by laying in the basic shapes, looking for middle tones but varying the colours so that they relate to the local colours of the objects. He starts with a limited palette of colours – raw umber, warm grey, cobalt, white, cadmium yellow and alizarin crimson – and works wet on wet, so that the colours melt together.*

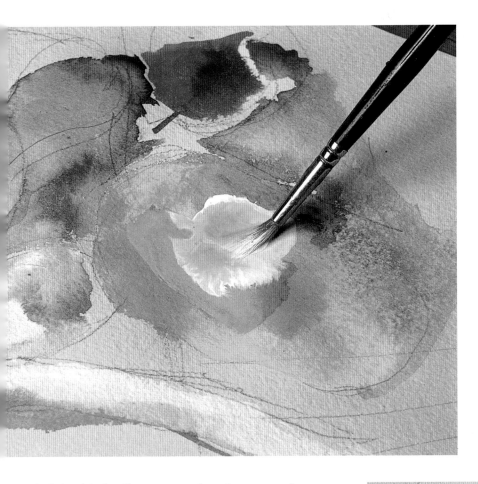

▽ **4** *This subject is complex and could be difficult. In the painting process several apparently contradictory activities are happening at any one time. You are working with the subject and also with the painting – both have contributions to make. Look carefully at each element of the subject, painting what you actually see rather than what you know to be there. Exaggerate and edit where necessary to make the painting 'work', but also be open to any 'happy accidents' that can be incorporated into the painting.*

△ **3** *In this detail you can see how important the warm mid-tone of the paper is. It provides a middle tone which holds the composition together and gives the artist a key to assess the lights and darks against. The texture of the paper is important too. See the way the brush has skipped across the surface so that the shadow cast by the coral has a broken edge. All these elements give a painting character.*

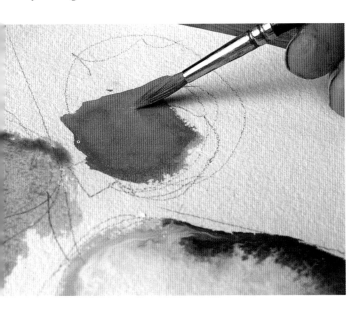

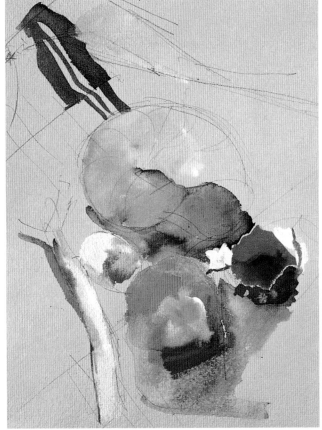

△ **5** *Here oil pastel is being used to create texture in certain passages. The dryish pastel skips across the paper surface, creating a pleasingly broken texture.*

△ **6** *Oil pastel was laid over the area of the sponge. Water is repelled by the oiliness, so when colour is washed over, it separates. You can see the way the colour has formed droplets.*

△ **7** *Don't be afraid to mix your media. In this passage you can see the way pink pastel has been used to create a rich, crusty texture on the lip of the murex shell and a resist on the sponge. The artist uses a warm grey that is both shadow and the dark side of the shell, and lays in just enough touches and a few pencil marks to define its frilly outline. In that way he has the best of both worlds: tonal values that are pleasing and work together, and a descriptive image.*

△ **8** *The 'piano key' cloth was a bit of a problem. There is a tendency to be too specific with a detailed element like this, but if you make this neater or more detailed than the rest of the painting, it will throw the whole work out of kilter. The artist approached the cloth boldly, first separating it into broad areas of light and dark and then working back with more lights into the darks. This is a good system which gives you a variety of shapes, tones and edges.*

◁ **9** *As the drawing emerges from the painting, remember that every line on the surface should contribute to the overall solidity of the piece. Here lines run around the forms and every mark, from the pinks of the murex shell on the right to the holes in the sponge, travels across the surface and helps describe the form.*

DAFFODILS

In this simple exploratory sketch the artist combines a wet-on-wet technique with oil-pastel resist. The subject is a bunch of vivid yellow daffodils in a blue papier-mâché jar. The blue of the pot and the yellow of the daffodils set each other off wonderfully. The decorative motif on the pot picks up the colour of the flowers, and there is an interesting contrast between the quality of the real and of the painted flowers. The blue vase has a very definite texture which gives it character. The oil-pastel resist provided the artist with a simple, direct and very fresh way of describing this.

Spend some time considering a subject before you dash in. Enjoy it and explore the colour and composition possibilities. Remember what it was about the subject that first caught your eye and try to get some of that into the work, whether it is a sketch, a watercolour or a big studio oil.

△ **2** *The artist started with a simple pencil drawing. Here he lays on a thin layer of blue oil pastel, which will 'resist' the watery wash of gouache.*

△ **1** *The bright yellow of the daffodils is marvellously set off by the brilliant blue of the jar.*

▷ **3** *He lays on the blue gouache – the reaction between the oily pastel and the watery paint causing the colour to separate, giving the area a texture that closely resembles the slightly knobbly surface of the pot.*

△ **4** *The flowers heads are laid in, using a wet-on-wet technique. Light and dark tones are used to give volume. A touch of Indian red is dotted into the centre to stand for the centres of the flowers.*

▽ **5** *The final colour sketch captures the brightness of the arrangement, the play of the blues and yellows and the surface qualities of the pot.*

TECHNIQUES

MASKING

There are many reasons why you may want to protect a section of the painting while you apply paint elsewhere. It might be that you wish to retain the colour of the paper to stand for the local colour of the subject, or you might want to save part of a painted area while you develop the rest of the painting. Masking allows you to work with considerable freedom, to paint the negative of a form – the space around a form – and also to introduce a variety of edges, giving a painting a special quality.

Masking with fluid

Masking fluid is a white or creamy liquid sold in small bottles. It is applied to the support with a brush or pen and dries to a rubbery film. You can then work over the masked areas, splashing paint around freely, confident that the masked paper will be protected. Masking fluid should be applied to virgin paper or paper that has been lightly tinted. Don't apply it over thick paint layers, as they may be disturbed when the mask is removed.

The mask can be removed once the paint layers are completely dry. Rub the film gently with your fingertips and the film will break up and come away from the paper as rubbery crumbs, revealing the pristine paper beneath.

Take a sheet of paper and apply masking fluid in as many ways as you can. Use a dip pen to make

Masking fluid was used to define the shape of the snake as well as the dots along its side. Masking allowed the artist to work freely while maintaining a crisp and neat outline.

dots and line, paint swirling lines and neat shapes with a brush and, using a loaded brush, flick on the fluid in a random way. Allow the mask to dry, then lay on a wash of colour. When the paint is dry, remove the masking fluid and see what you've got. You'll notice that masking fluid gives you crisply defined edges.

Masking with tape

You can use low-tack tape to create neat edges and lines. Stick masking tape to the support, apply paint in the usual way and when the paint is dry lift the tape to reveal neat bands of unpainted paper.

Paper masks

Torn paper can be used to create loose masks, which can be used to protect large areas while you

Masking fluid
▷ *Masking fluid was applied with a brush. When it was dry a wash of colour was laid on and allowed to dry. Here we see the rubbery film being removed, revealing the clean paper beneath. Notice the crisp edges of the painted areas.*

work elsewhere. Their primary function, though, is to create a range of interesting edges. Take a selection of different papers – some thick, some thin – and tear them in strips. Compare the results and you'll find that different papers tear in different ways. This quality can be exploited in your work. You could tear a paper mask for a tree or a hedge in a landscape, then lay on paint boldly. When you lift the mask the silhouette of the feature will be revealed. You will have painted the negative.

TECHNIQUES

USING GUM ARABIC

Both watercolour and gouache consist of pigment bound with gum arabic – a water-soluble adhesive produced by several species of acacia tree. Gum arabic is also used as a painting medium – that is, a substance which modifies the way paint behaves. Gum arabic is readily available as a honey-coloured liquid; gum water is a more dilute form of the same substance.

The uses of gum arabic

Gum arabic performs several functions. It extends the paint, that is it makes it go further. If you thin paint with water, you will dilute the colour and also reduce its viscosity, so that it flows easily over the paper. By adding gum arabic, you can dilute the colour while retaining some of its substance, so the paint is more easily controlled and holds marks. Gum arabic acts like a varnish, giving the paint a slight sheen and keeping the colours bright and fresh. It is particularly useful for building up textures, and its 'gumminess' allows you to scratch into the paint surface, while its adhesive qualities mean that, once dry, the paint holds these marks.

Working with gum arabic

It is very difficult to convey just how paint 'feels' to handle, yet the painting process is all about

▷ *Gum arabic was added to mixed pinks and mauves and then used to sponge on the flower heads.*

◁ *Here, the artist works into the paint surface with the tip of a brush handle. The viscosity of the gum arabic means that the paint retains these marks, creating a complex web of subtle textures.*

responses, and more particularly your enjoyment of the paint, the paper and the paint surface. You set off with a particular intention, but the way the paper takes the paint, or the way the brush feels as it glides or drags across the paper surface, elicits a response in you. So, the quality of the materials has a direct influence on the end product.

What I am saying yet again is that you'll just have to have a go yourself. Put some gum arabic in a dish, mix it with paint and work it over the surface. You'll find that the paint becomes quite frothy, but most of the bubbles disperse as the paint dries, though some passages will be speckled. You can work into the paint surface at any stage until it is dry. Some of the best effects are achieved when it is just tacky.

PROJECTS

LAMP

In this study of an oil lamp and its reflection in a window, masking fluid was used to retain the white of the paper in the area of the two light globes. By retaining the white of the paper, the artist was able to achieve a good, sparkling transparency later on. It also meant that he was working with negative forms, with the space around the globes, rather than with the globes themselves. This approach, working light on dark and dark on light, plus working positive and negative, gives the work an abstract feeling which is rather attractive. It is an interesting way of making a picture.

The other challenging aspect of this group is the reflective transparency of the paraffin-filled reservoir and the brass of the stand. The artist starts with a combination of a wet-on-wet underpainting in which he uses warm and cool versions of the related colours. In the blue reservoir there is a cool blue and a hotter, purply blue. In the lamp base there is a yellow and a cool greenish yellow. Crisp dabs, patches and streaks of colour are added later to build up the reflective, light-scattering surfaces.

The whole painting is developed at the same pace, constantly making adjustments to ensure that colours and tones retain a meaningful relationship. For example, the earthy red used to lay on the warm shadows on the oranges is picked up in the windowsill, in the reflections on the brass, in the reservoir and even in the warmish tinge to the glass at the top of the painting. In this way the eye is led across and around the picture area. The image has a sense of coherence, a wholeness, with the separate elements working in unison.

Compositionally, the final image works on several levels. The main elements are the verticals of the glazing bars and the angles of the sills – all lead towards the lamp. The globes themselves occupy an important position just off-centre of the picture area. If you half close your eyes, you can see the image in terms of its tonal arrangements. The lightest tones are the globes, but there is a paleness

around that area. The warm yellow tones of the reflected globe, the lamp base and the oranges provide another theme in the central area.

△ 1 *The lamp and its reflection, and the glittering surfaces of the metal base and the glass reservoir, are the subject of this painting. With a difficult subject, the best approach is to start by simplifying it, working towards a more complex image.*

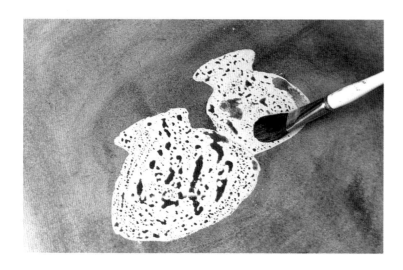

◁ **3** *He made a very simple pencil drawing and then applied masking fluid over the silhouette of the 'globes'. When the masking fluid was dry, a grey-blue mix was washed on.*

▽ **4** *The broad forms of the image are washed in. You will have to concentrate hard to reduce the main areas of colour and tone to their simplest forms. Half closing your eyes will exaggerate the tonal contrasts and help you to focus on them. Remember that you are establishing a base upon which you can add your elaborations.*

▽ **2** *The artist made an annotated colour sketch of the lamp globe and its reflection. The colours in this area were subtle and had to be rendered faithfully if the image was to succeed. Subjects like this need careful handling to avoid any crudeness. It helps to talk yourself through the colour relationships, as this forces you to be analytical.*

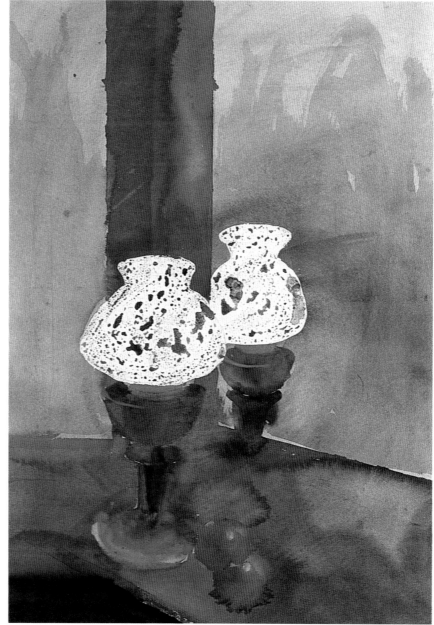

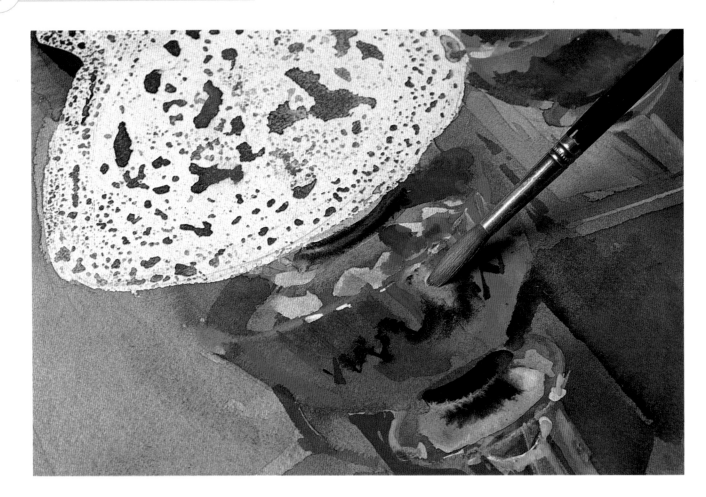

△ **5** *Patches of opaque colour are added to create the sparkle of the glass. Paint what you actually see and keep the work fresh. Don't fiddle or overwork the paint. Stand back from the painting at regular intervals to check progress. It is only at a distance that you can really judge the effectiveness of any passage.*

◁ **6** *Compare this stage with the painting on the previous page. You will find that darker tones have been introduced at the top so that the image is enclosed and attention is drawn back to the focal point. The objects have been developed with a range of tones, and highlights have been applied freshly and directly.*

▷ **7** *The film of masking fluid was peeled off, revealing the white paper beneath. A pale wash of warm colour was applied to the glass globe. A cool blue at the base and around the rim gives it form, and crisp white paint highlights the rim where it catches the light. The reflected lamp is handled in a similar way, but the colours are warmer and more solid.*

PROJECTS

FIGURE

Portraiture and figure painting are fascinating topics for the artist and are endlessly satisfying. Ideally, start by working from a posed figure. Perhaps you can persuade a friend or a family member to sit for you.

Spend some time arranging the model, assessing the shapes, colours and tones and the dynamics within the composition. Get the model to take up different poses, make some rapid sketches and try different compositions. Will it be head only, head and shoulders, full figure, seated, standing, full face, side or three-quarters view? Consider the clothing. Do the colours contribute to the composition? Do they reflect the qualities in the sitter that you want to bring out? Fabrics are important. Some drape and reveal the underlying forms, while others are bulky and conceal form – both are interesting.

The first thing to bear in mind is that a figure or portrait is just another subject to be composed and interpreted in terms of tones, colours and textures. People are sometimes rather tentative about figure or portrait painting, worried by the end product and the problem of getting a likeness. Forget the likeness and concentrate on all the other aspects of picture making. You'll find that a likeness is actually not that difficult to achieve, but let it come out of the other factors.

What is really difficult to get is the spirit of the individual – the set of the shoulders, the tilt of the neck, the shape of the hands, the length of the arms. Measure everything very carefully, comparing the size of the hands with the size of the head, constantly assessing one feature against another, and using your pencil (see page 88) to measure angles and distances. All these separate elements will add up to the unique individual. If you get them right, you will capture something of the personality behind them.

1 *The artist started by exploring different poses. The one in which the model looks out of the picture, hands crossed, has interesting internal dynamics – the relationship between hands and head, the compact angles of the torso and the way her gaze is directed beyond the picture.*

▷ **2** *The artist started laying in some rather generalized lines in charcoal on good-quality watercolour paper – charcoal can be dusted off and won't muddy the colour. A small hand-mirror is a useful way of checking the drawing. When you see the image in reverse it throws up inconsistencies, because you are seeing it in an unfamiliar way. It is particularly useful when you are not seeing the figure absolutely head on.*

▷ **3** *Charcoal dust was removed from the surface by flicking it lightly with a duster. Then colour was laid in, working boldly, finding the main areas of light and dark.*

▽ 4 *As you can see, the artist has worked very generally and boldly, using a wet-on-wet technique. The structural lines of the drawing still show through the thin paint layer. Keep on checking that the perspective works, that the chair is solid and that there is enough room for the thigh, the lower leg and the knee. Remember that the figure is solid and be aware of the other side of things, and the connections between, say, the thigh and the hip, the thigh and the chair seat. You must imply the existence of the parts you cannot see.*

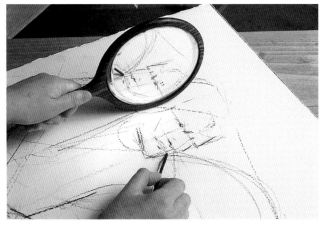

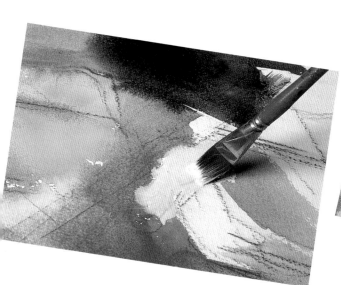

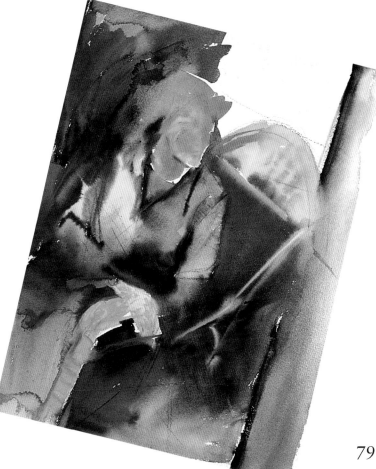

▷ **5** *Details are added, darker tones to give form to the hair, and light and dark tones on the face and as an indication of the features. Avoid the temptation to pay too much attention to the head and keep the marks crisp and loose.*

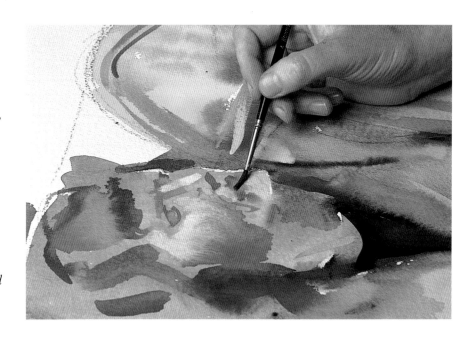

▽ **6** *The form is beginning to emerge from the paper. Keep on checking the structures and perspective. Stand back from the support and view both the figure and the painting through half-closed eyes. This will allow you to concentrate on the tones.*

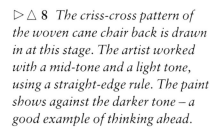

▽ **7** *Masking tape is used to define the arms of the chair so that a smooth line can be achieved.*

▷△ **8** *The criss-cross pattern of the woven cane chair back is drawn in at this stage. The artist worked with a mid-tone and a light tone, using a straight-edge rule. The paint shows against the darker tone – a good example of thinking ahead.*

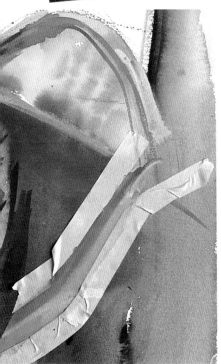

▷ **9** *A wash of blue knocks back the background. Light and dark tones and warm and cools can be harnessed to describe the form and give it solidity.*

You will need to phase the painting to allow the model breaks every so often – more regularly for a standing than for a seated figure. Use chalk to mark the position of the feet on the floor. Masking tape can be used on chairs and fabrics to record the position of other limbs. But be prepared to make some adjustments as the painting progresses – the pose always changes slightly.

△ **10** *The hair should be treated as a solid element with volume. Again, use lights and darks to express this, but avoid the temptation to be too neat or precise. Similarly, the face should be seen in terms of tones.*

◁ **11** *Oil pastel is used to add linear elements and texture.*

▷ **12** *In the final painting there is plenty of entertainment in the composition – in the repeated curves of the chair, the relationship of the figure to the chair and the background, and the way she gazes across and out of the painting. The paint surface is full of interest too, from the subtle modulations of colour in the sitter's garment, to the energetic treatment of the hair, and to the decorative elements in the wicker chair.*

PROJECTS

ANEMONES

As an artist you have to keep on challenging yourself, setting yourself new tasks and exercises. In this way you will always be learning and you will keep your approach fresh and avoid lapsing into easy formulae. If you always use oil, try watercolour or acrylic. If you paint on a small scale, make yourself do something large. If you favour landscapes, try a still life, a figure study or a self-portrait. Collage is a marvellous medium. It can be used either as part of serious mixed-media work or for studies or exercises. Its great advantage is that it removes your 'handwriting' – you must cut or tear the paper, and this forces you to be bold in your interpretation of the subject.

You can use coloured papers, tissue, fabric, acetate, almost anything; you can also tone papers or paint them with bold textures.

Have a go. Choose a simple image which engages you. Work quickly, enjoy the process and try not to make heavy weather of it. It is the process, the 'doing', which is important, rather than the finished image. Set yourself an exercise like this from time to time. You'll find it refreshing and interesting.

△ **2** *The support is a piece of card. The approach is exactly the same as for any other painting. The main shapes were laid in, working briskly, with the edge of a plastic palette knife. Paper was torn and glued with gum. Further details were added with paint.*

△ **1** *These brightly coloured anemones are a lovely subject and are ideal for a bold collage approach.*

▷ **3** *More colour and paper are added, working quickly, always looking for tonal relationships.*

△ **4** *The combination of paper, painting, torn edges, dabs and dashes of colour and line work is pleasing.*

5 *The warm textured grey of the card provides a useful mid-tone which holds the image together and provides a key against which the lights and darks tell. Paint, paper, pastel and pencil combine to create an image which, though simple, is descriptive and entertaining.*

85

PROJECTS

SKULL

Here we look at a very small object. Scale is an important aspect of painting or drawing, and the size of this object means that you must work quite close to it in order to see it properly.

The scale at which you work is important too. When you work on a large scale at an easel, you use bold gestures from the shoulder; closer to, you use movements from the elbow. A small drawing like this will exploit neat, restrained gestures from the wrist. The way you work dictates the sort of line you make and the energy that you put into it. Whether you are standing or sitting will also affect the marks you make and your approach. It is much easier to make big, sweeping marks when you are standing at an easel and working with a long-handled brush. Sitting at a table and working with pencil, you are likely to be more constrained and focused. It is useful to work deliberately on a different scale from time to time.

At this scale you have to focus your attention, because there is nothing apart from the object to distract you. This sort of focused drawing and painting is a marvellous way of sharpening your powers of observation. Really examine the object, study it, hold it, look at it from every angle and try to understand how it works. Having got to know the object, set it on a surface so that you can see it and draw it without moving your head. Your eyes should be able to move between object and paper surface and back easily and without any other movements. In that way you can really concentrate.

△ 1 *This bird's skull is a beautiful object, alarmingly light and extremely complicated. The artist set himself up so that he was comfortable, close to the object and could see it by merely moving his eyes. He worked on watercolour paper with a soft pencil.*

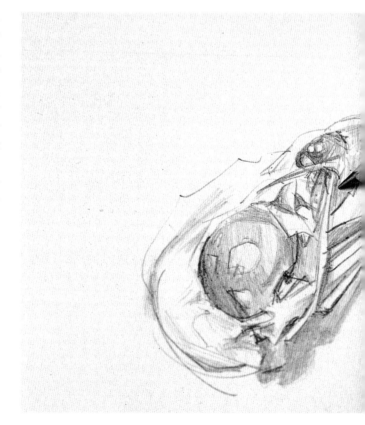

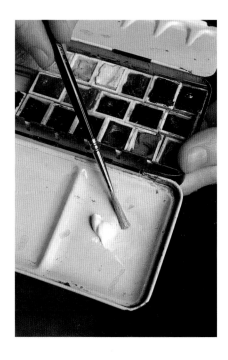

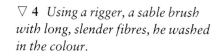

◁ **3** *He laid on colour with body colour – watercolour with white added to make it opaque.*

▽ **4** *Using a rigger, a sable brush with long, slender fibres, he washed in the colour.*

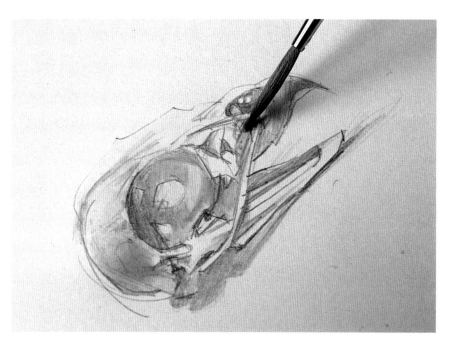

▽ **2** *He made the drawing by looking for edges, for areas of dark and light tone, and by measuring one shape against another. The spaces between elements and the spaces around the object, even the shape of the shadow, are important.*

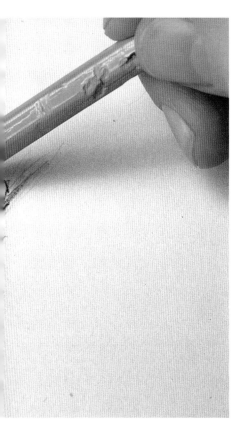

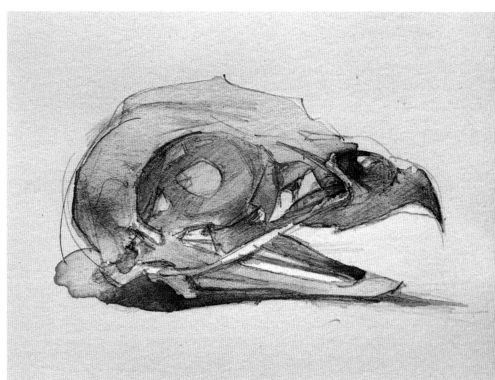

△ **5** *A mixture of white and raw sienna is used to tint the skull, then black is washed into the shadow, particularly beneath the skull.*

PROJECTS

FARMHOUSE

This is a fairly ambitious project because dealing with the perspective problems of buildings is difficult, especially for the beginner. The theory of linear perspective is complicated, but you can make a picture work simply by drawing what you see. By measuring and establishing accurately the relationships between the elements in the landscape, you will be able to produce a drawing which convinces. Your pencil is a useful measuring tool – hold it in front of you at arm's length and study the subject through half-closed eyes. Here, for example, you would look at the run of farm buildings on the top of the sheet. You can establish that the total length of the roof is six times the height of the wall from footing to eaves. In the same way, by holding your pencil up you can ascertain the angles of the building which we see in three-quarters view in the drawing below.

The other factor which made this a difficult subject was the wide angle of the view. The artist wanted to include the whole building. This would have been difficult to achieve with a camera, but an artist has more licence to edit out walls and trees which in nature would impede the view.

The artist used pen and ink for the initial drawing, adding colour with washes of gouache. He then used a variety of mixed-media techniques, including wax resist and pencil, to achieve the interestingly weathered textures of the rough stone walls.

There are other problems which were unique to this particular painting session. It was February and the weather was very changeable – brilliant sunshine one moment and spring showers the next. The artist had to keep dashing in and out. He used a large sheet of heavy watercolour paper, unstretched and pinned to a board. He painted both views of the building on the same sheet so that he could keep both paintings going at the same time.

△ **1** *The artist started by drawing the main outlines of the building and the composition in pencil, measuring lines and angles against each other, dropping perpendiculars and horizontals to make sure that everything fell into its correct place. He then started to tighten up the drawing with Indian ink and pen. He washed in colour at quite an early stage.*

△ **2** *These paintings are rather large, so I've pulled out a section of the bottom one to allow you to study progress. Here you can see the way pencil, ink and colour are building up. Notice the way the texture of the wall is created by loosely applied transparent washes. Some of the white areas are created by a wax resist. The artist has used a sponge to apply colour and create texture in the area of the shrub.*

△ **3** *Washes of colour are laid on the roof, with a second, darker, wash for the cast shadow. Detail has been added to the dovecot.*

▽ **4** *A pinkish-ochery soft pastel gives warmth to the stonework.*

▷ **5** *The artist kept the whole painting going at the same time. It is important not to get distracted by one area if you want the tonal arrangements within the painting to make sense and to retain satisfying colour relationships. Each part of the painting must work, but, more importantly, it should also succeed as a whole.*

▽ **6** *Washes of cool grey have been laid over the roof and on the wall to pull the whole image together and to prevent it being too 'dancy'. The foreground is completed and touches of bright blue in the dark areas enliven the shadows.*

△ **7** With loose pencil lines, the main structures and relationships are established. Colour is then flooded in and allowed to bleed and blend. To create a sky, simply damp the paper and dot in mixed colour, then leave it to spread. If the result isn't right, you can either wipe it off and start again or add more colour, move the paint about a bit, or use a sponge or a tissue to blot it off.

▽ **8** The picture has travelled a long way from the stage above. The colour is freely handled. The artist's approach here differs from that on the facing page – it is less tight, with fewer drawn lines, but captures the character of the building and the surrounding landscape.

PROJECTS

MILL

In this painting the artist added gum arabic to the paint. Gum arabic is the vehicle which holds the particles of pigment in watercolour and gouache paint. It is also used as a medium – that is, a substance which alters the way that the paint behaves. It works in three ways. It is a gummy glue-like substance which, when added to the paint, allows you to work textures into the paint. It also thins the paint and gives it a more transparent quality, like a varnish or a glaze. Finally, it gives the colour extra sparkle and freshness.

The artist started by toning the ground with a warm earth colour. Over that he blocked in areas of colour, looking for positive tonal contrasts to give him something to work against. He developed the whole picture surface, looking for descriptions of the view, but allowing himself to play with the colours and textures of the paint, especially in the water. There he exploited the many qualities of gum arabic, giving the paint extra transparency, scratching back into its thickened, gummy surface with a knife to reveal the colours beneath. The gum gives the colours an extra brilliance and sheen which are in sympathy with the water.

This project illustrates the licence you can take with gouache. You can splash the paint around, handling it with joyous abandon, enjoying its qualities and simply seeing what happens. This approach provides a glorious arena for 'happy accidents': the unpredictable puddling and melting of colours, paint drying to give hard tidemarks and strange textures – things which give a painting excitement and edge if you are brave enough to allow them to happen.

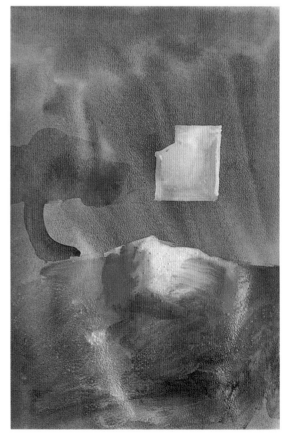

Here the artist has worked very freely to create colour and atmosphere, then pulled the painting into focus by adding carefully observed and judiciously placed details. This is a marvellous way of working, especially with landscape. The tension between the expressive and the descriptive elements gives the painting a compelling internal energy.

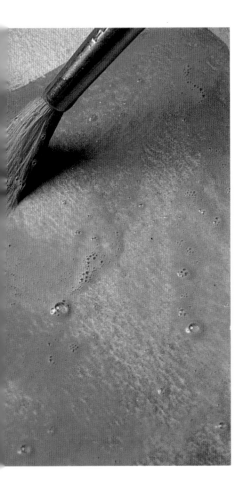

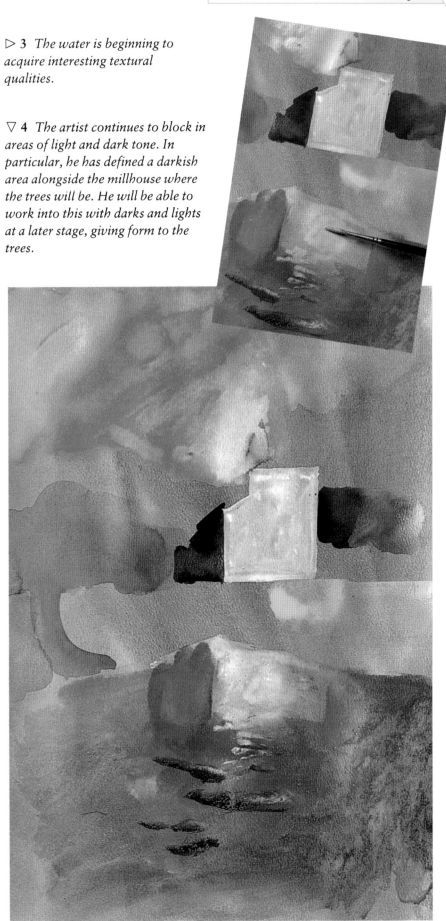

▷ **3** *The water is beginning to acquire interesting textural qualities.*

▽ **4** *The artist continues to block in areas of light and dark tone. In particular, he has defined a darkish area alongside the millhouse where the trees will be. He will be able to work into this with darks and lights at a later stage, giving form to the trees.*

△ **1** *The background was toned with a warm earth colour. The artist then started to block in the main areas of tone. This is a useful way of simplifying a complex subject. Here he is laying white tinted with blue and mixed with gum arabic to give it a transparent clarity.*

◁ **2** *The area where the water in the foreground will be is laid in using loosely scumbled colour. The warm toning is allowed to show through. The gum holds the water on the paper surface and also retains the gestural brushmarks. These will contribute to the final watery effects.*

▷ 5 *The side of a palette knife is used to lay in streaks of solid colour.*

▷ 6 *With the tip of the knife, the artist scratches into the paint surface. Gum arabic allows you plenty of opportunity for this sort of playfulness.*

▽ 7 *Here the artist is working into the wooded area which he established earlier. He picks up the lights and holds the background. Interestingly, the trees are described as darks on lights in the area of the sky, and lights on darks here, creating a striking counterpoint.*

△ 8 *Here you can see the way in which the image has been reduced to lights and darks, simply and directly rendered. The texture of the paper also contributes a subtle texture to the images, breaking through the films of colour, so that even flat washes have some texture.*

The underpainting gives the picture an underlying warmth. It also pushes the water in the foreground forward and implies levels and depths. The texture in this area fulfils two functions: it draws the eye and helps define the frontal plane of the image, and it gives the painting character.

A landscape should work in two ways. You should be able to read the surface of the painting and your eye should travel around it, finding passages that demand further attention, and then passing on again without losing the viewer's attention.

95

INDEX

A
Acrylic 6
    media 17, 46
Aerial perspective 32, *44*

B
Body colour 15
Brushes 20
    cleaning of *27*

C
Candle wax resist 58
    use of *58*
Card (as support) *84*
Cardboard 58
Collage 84
Crayons, wax 58

D
Dabbing off 56
Dabbing on 56
Daler Rowney 14
Dark-on-light technique 34
Drawing boards 23
Dry-brush techniques 26, 27, 57
Drying times 8

E
Easels 22

F
Fibreboard 18

Figure painting 78

G
Gouache
    advantages of 6, 35
    approaches to 10
    'designers' 4
    qualities of 8
Gum arabic, use of 72, 73, 92

H
Hairdryer, use of *37*
Holtam, Brenda 7, 9, 11

L
Landscape painting 42, 95
Light-on-dark technique 34
Linear perspective 88

M
Masking 70, 71
    fluid 22, 70, *71*, 74
    tape 23, 71
Masks, paper 71
Media 22
    mixing of 8, 66
Mood 33

O
Oil pastel 59, 66, 68, 82
    resist *59*, 68

P
Paint surface
    quality of *50*
    use of 26, 27
Painting knife, use of *44*
Paints 14, 15
Palette knife, use of 94
Palettes 23
    for figure work 27
    for landscape 27
    limited 27
Paper
    coloured 16
    hot-pressed 16
    stretching 18
    suitable for gouache *16, 17*
    tinted 10, *45*
    watercolour 16
    weight of 17
    wrapping 58
Perspective
    aerial 32, *44*
    linear 88
Portraiture 78
Poster colour 15

R
Resist techniques 58

S
Scale 8, 86

Smith, Adrian 7, 9
Smith, Stan 5, 7, 11, 37, 40, 54, 64
Spattering 56
Still-life painting 64
Supports 16, 17

T
Taylor, William 9
Texture 54
    creating 56, 57
Toning ground 10, 40, 92
    support for 10, 40
    with brush *40*
    with sponge *41*
Tube colour *26*

U
Underpainting *95*

W
Wash
    flat 28
    laying of 28
Watercolour
    board 50
    opaque 4
    pure 6, 36
    techniques for 8
    transparent 6, 15
Wet on dry 31
Wet on wet 30, 68, 74